BREAKING YOUR TIME BARRIERS

BECOMING A STRATEGIC TIME MANAGER

Ross Arkell Webber

The Wharton School
University of Pennsylvania

Prentice Hall, Englewood Cliffs, New Jersey 07632

Library of Congress Cataloging-in-Publication Data

Webber, Ross A.
    Breaking your time barriers : becoming a strategic time manager /
    Ross Arkell Webber.
        p.   cm.
    ISBN 0-13-085374-7
    1. Time management.   I. Title.
HD69. T54W434   1991
658.4'093—dc20   91-12387
                                                                 CIP

Editorial/production supervision
  and interior design: *bookworks*
Copy Editor: *Karen Verde*
Cover design: *Lundgren Graphics, Ltd.*
Prepress buyer: *Kelly Behr*
Manufacturing buyer: *Susan Brunke*
Acquisition editor: *John Willig*

Title page cartoon reprinted with special permission of King Features
Syndicate.

 Published by Prentice-Hall, Inc.
A Simon & Schuster Company
Englewood Cliffs, New Jersey 07632

The publisher offers discounts on this book when ordered
in bulk quantities. For more information, write:
    Special Sales/College Marketing
    Prentice-Hall, Inc.
    College Technical and Reference Division
    Englewood Cliffs, NJ 07632

Printed in the United States of America

10 9 8 7 6 5 4 3 2 1

ISBN   0-13-085374-7

Prentice-Hall International (UK) Limited, *London*
Prentice-Hall of Australia Pty. Limited, *Sydney*
Prentice-Hall Canada Inc., *Toronto*
Prentice-Hall Hispanoamericana, S.A., *Mexico*
Prentice-Hall of India Private Limited, *New Delhi*
Prentice-Hall of Japan, Inc., *Tokyo*
Simon & Schuster Asia Pte. Ltd., *Singapore*
Editora Prentice-Hall do Brasil, Ltda., *Rio de Janeiro*

TO

CLARENCE WALTON
LEONARD SAYLES
SHELDON HACKNEY
REGINALD JONES

With Thanks for Helping Me at Various Points in My Life
to Devote My Time to Important Objectives

CONTENTS

INTRODUCTION

Former Connecticut Governor, Cabinet Secretary, and United States Senator Abraham Ribicoff was one of the most effective time managers with whom I've ever worked. I once asked him why his senatorial office seemed so efficient, effective, and even tranquil in contrast to the seeming chaos of most of his Washington colleagues. He replied that it was because at 70 years of age he was not running for president and that he had told his constituents that he was a political wholesaler, not a retailer!

Ribicoff's explanation captures the essence of effective time management by those who are able to break the time barrier. Not being a presidential candidate meant that rather than keeping up with *everything*, he could focus on those objectives that his experience-born wisdom told him were important; and "wholesaling" rather than "retailing" meant that his time was devoted to longer run, more important goals rather than frittered away on small problems.

No one can ignore immediate time demands and present tasks, of course, but the key for effective strategic time managers is satisfactorily completing such tasks while protecting time and energy to project themselves into the future and push ahead on more important longer range objectives. One of the most characteristic behaviors of time barrier breakers is sitting on the toilet while looking through their pocket calendars for next week and next month. Although not a particularly elevating vision, it is an elevating activity, for such a ponderer is projecting himself/ herself into the future and playing with time management scenarios— what can I start today so that next month's deadline won't mean a later all-night panic.

This workbook is designed to assist you in this longer run time management. Rather than offering another form for today's "to do list," It presents a series of exercises intended to help you define what is most important to you and your organization and to gain discretionary time to focus on these more deferrable objectives. Your concern should be less with time management tactics than strategies. All of these exercises have been developed and used with hundreds of participants over the past 15 years in numerous corporate management development programs and in my Wharton program in Executive Self-Management.

Forms are provided on which to complete each exercise. In addition, each is illustrated with a real example, some drawn from my own experience as a university vice president and others from my consulting experiences with executives and even United States Senators. A discussion containing an illustration follows the description of the exercise. Feel free to peek ahead to the discussion before or while you are completing the exercise. Because they deal with the fundamental and the long run, some of the exercises in this book will take substantial time to complete. Nonetheless, you should be able to complete all of them within a month.

At the end of the book is a master daily time and activity planning form which you might reproduce for use during the year. The form is designed to integrate your response and discretionary activities along with to do lists of your most dominant tasks as well as your investments in longer run, more deferrable objectives.

In between each exercise is a short discussion of a time management theme to keep in mind as you attempt to improve your strategic time management (along with cartoons to remind you of the need for a bit of modesty and humor as you deal with life's uncertainties).

And **now** is a good time to begin. Good luck.

Ross A. Webber

ON SPINACH LOVERS
AND HATERS
TACTICS FOR FIGHTING
PROCRASTINATION

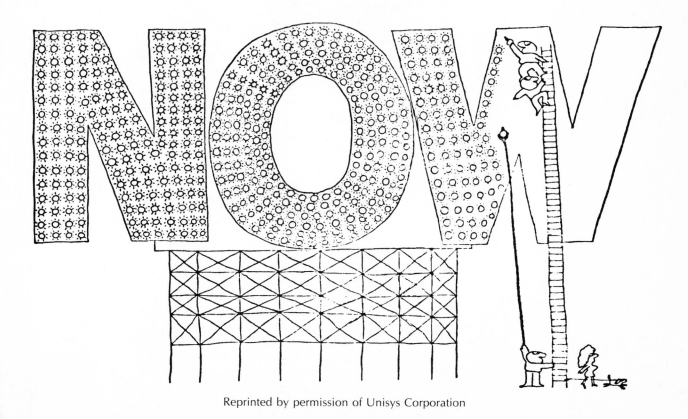

When you were a child, did you eat your spinach first or last? It could have been cauliflower or broccoli, but most everyone had some vegetable they just hated to eat. Nonetheless, many of us had parents who enforced a rule of no bread or dessert until *all* of the main course was eaten, including the dreaded vegetable.

Assuming you really wanted that sweet reward at dinner's end, your two polar choices were to eat the spinach first and then be home free or save it until last, just before the ice cream. No data exist on what percentage opts for either course, but the dilemma is suggestive of time management. Effective time managers seem to consume the spinach of their jobs first.

In contrast, procrastinators put off the spinach in hope that the demanding parents will relax their guard and forget to enforce the rule. Such delay works sometimes of course, but probably rarely. Procrastination stems from complex causes that may well require a Freudian's couch to unravel. We can't do that here, but we can describe some tactics to combat it.

1. Set deadlines to begin. This can appear to be an excuse for delaying rather than starting immediately. But not every task can be started now, so deadlines are appropriate. Of course you can lead yourself to water, but you must also force yourself to begin.

2. Generate momentum. Some people have trouble starting a task—any task— especially in the morning or after lunch. A tough, ambiguous, deferrable procrastinable task can be extremely discouraging. Momentum can be developed, however, by beginning with some easy, programmed tasks like routine correspondence and bureaucratic detail. But set a time limit on how long you will do this and stick to it. A desk alarm set for 30 minutes will signal you to stop the easy and start the difficult. Don't be sucked in by the sense of achievement you may feel from completing the routine tasks. Give them up after a half hour. Confront the ambiguous.

3. Reward yourself for progress. All big complex projects have smaller parts that can be celebrated as they are accomplished. Small self-rewards like a coffee break or even an afternoon off to play golf *are* justified if they mark significant progress on a lengthy project. Just be scrupulously honest with yourself that they follow and not precede or replace the actual work.

4. Include others in rewards. One of the sad aspects of modern work life is that it is divorced from family life. Children and spouse may not even know when wife, husband, Mom, or Dad has accomplished something significant on the job. Perhaps you could invite them into a small dinnertime ritual. Have a little ceremony; tell of your progress and of your ultimate goal. Give yourself a small gift that can be shared with other family members. And thank them for their implicit support of your work. After awhile, they may begin to share more with you and the exchange of small rewards will be more mutual.

5. Discount in advance. No one is *perfectly honest* with him or herself. Even the healthiest of us utilize certain games or neuroticisms to deal with difficulty. Discounting means imaginatively projecting yourself into the future before the completion of the task and in advance dealing with inevitable disappointment. Then when the job is actually completed you will have already worked through the letdown that the result is not exactly as you wished. A certain fatalism characterizes this technique, of course, but it is not crippling if you feel that for the most part the results reflect not chance but your effort. It is just a pre-recognition that you are not omnipotent and that perfection is impossible.

The moral of the spinach tale is that effective time management usually includes the courage to confront the difficult and unpleasant early, sooner rather than later. In high school, nonprocrastinators may have started Saturday's chores on Friday afternoon, thus gaining flexibility if something interesting turned up in the morning. In college they probably tried to get at least a solid hour of afternoon study in before dinner (worth probably two hours of late night time).

Effective time managers seldom accept other people's deadlines, *but create artificial deadlines that are sooner*. Although this would seem to increase the pressure on them, paradoxically such self-set artificial deadlines seem to have the opposite effect. They create the illusion of being a little more in control of time. They know they have a little leeway beyond the artificial deadline, but they almost never use it.

In short, effective time managers try to act on time rather than passively letting it just happen *to* them. No one is entirely successful at this, but the effort seems to strengthen one's self-control, which makes the battle easier.

Exercise One

BEING AWARE
OF THE DANGERS
FOR AMBITIOUS PEOPLE

OBJECTIVES

- to be aware of how your personality affects your perception of time
- to recognize how your drive to use time well and be efficient in the short run can lead to long-run ineffectiveness

"You'd damn well better come up with an antidote before five o'clock, Stimson. This project has cost enough without having to pay you overtime."

A. EXERCISE—PERCEIVING TIME

Answer the following questions:

1. Which of the following images more closely fits time in your life?
   - a quiet motionless ocean? ___
   - a galloping horse and rider? ___

2. Which two of the following words best describes the idea of time for you?

sharp	___	empty	___
sad	___	tense	___
active	___	active	___
soothing	___	clear	___
cold	___	deep	___

3. How many years have passed since each of the following events?
   - resignation of President Nixon ___ years
   - U.S. invasion of Panama ___ years
   - end of Vietnam War ___ years
   - Iraq's invasion of Iran ___ years
   - The New York Yankees won
     the baseball world series ___ years

4. Find a quiet room where you will not be disturbed. You should not have a watch, clock, radio, television, or anything to read or work on. You will just sit. Before you closet yourself, have a friend agree to call you after a period of time he determines (not longer than an hour!). Now go sit. When your friend calls, estimate how much time has passed while you were sitting in the room.
   - your estimate: ___ minutes
   - actual time: ___ minutes

5. Check your wristwatch for accuracy. Use the radio or telephone to determine the exact time.
   - your watch time ___
   - correct time ___

B. DISCUSSION—THE DANGERS FOR ACHIEVEMENT-ORIENTED PEOPLE

The previous tests have been given to many people, particularly to determine their need for achievement. People high in this need tend to share certain perspectives on time and to gravitate toward careers like management. They crave the satisfaction of completing difficult tasks through persistent effort, of reaching a distant goal by moderately risky action.

Movement, direction, and value characterize such individuals' views on time. Most people with high achievement needs choose a metaphor like "a galloping horse and rider" rather than "a quiet motionless ocean." Complementing this dynamic perspective, they more frequently describe time in energy implicit words like "sharp," "active," and "tense" rather than "empty," "soothing," or "sad."

People with high achievement needs seem more acutely aware of time's passage. They tend to recall past events as nearer the present than they are by underestimating the time that has passed—perhaps because they have been so busy doing things. The actual dates for the events listed are:

- Resignation of President Nixon: August 1974
- U.S. invasion of Panama: December 1989
- End of Vietnam War: April 1975
- Iraq's invasion of Iran: September 1980
- The New York Yankees won the baseball world series: October 1978

When sitting alone in an isolated room, however, high achievement-oriented people tend to overestimate how much time has passed. Indeed, they frequently become nervous and a bit angry, concerned that the precious sands of time are sifting through their fingers, lost forever.

Finally, such ambitious people tend to have watches that are fast! More precisely, they have set their watches (and alarm clocks) ahead a bit attempting to *create* time, a little game to delude themselves that they are getting ahead of tyrannical time. In a real sense, achievement-oriented people (and most users of this workbook) are *time-haunted*.

I have great admiration for such people. Such motivation is extremely helpful to personal success and effectiveness; it is essential for an organization to have a cadre of such professionals and managers, and is even vital for the survival of a nation and culture. Nonetheless, being a time-haunted, achievement-oriented person carries some dangers about which you should be aware.

Overemphasis on Self: In their haste to use time efficiently, such people need to fight the inclination to express a kind of "God Complex." This is the tendency of ambitious people to place themselves in the center of the universe so that *their* time is more valuable than others', *their* time is the only one that is correct, and *they* alone are justified in being unpunctual. Such behavior treats others as objects or tools rather than human beings, with their subsequent resentment of being manipulated by your Machiavellian tactics. Unfortunately, achievement-oriented people are particularly prone to Machiavellianism with its inevitable cost in political goodwill. You shall see warnings in some of the following exercises of the need to carve time out of the busy present to invest in graciously responding to people and to building longer term relationships.

Tyranny of the Present: The very business of ambitious people allows the immediate to dominate their time. Days fractionated into two-minute events with the longest uninterrupted alone time as short as eight- to ten-minute intervals force them to fall into a busy but essentially passive mode of responding to telephone calls, visitors, and meetings as they come. Overly concerned with immediate measurable results and fearful of the ambiguity of less quantifiable objectives, achievement-oriented individuals sort of sleepwalk through their careers without visualizing a different future. Some exercises are reminders of the critical need to escape periodically from the present to invest in the future.

Repetition of the Past: The tragic result of short-run success for many, is that these people begin to repeat themselves. They respond to new cues as if they were the same as the past. But the new cues may be different, a difference they don't see because of an enjoyment of familiar behavior and satisfaction with past results. Success in a narrow speciality particularly exposes this type to the risk of losing sensitivity to how the nearer professional world and further external environment are changing. Our exercises will end with a means for encouraging oneself to periodically let go of the comfortable routine and confront ambiguity on and off the job.

ON BEING PREPARED
USING UNEXPECTED
GIFTS OF TIME

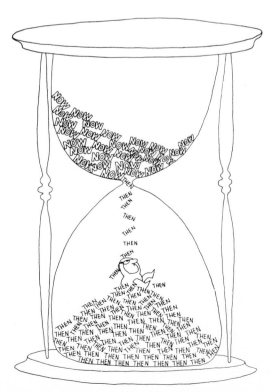

Reprinted by permission of Unisys Corporation.

Waiting for someone usually provokes anger in ambitious people. We fret over the lost time because we basically agree with Ben Franklin's Poor Richard that "time is money" and "a waste of time is the worst of sins." Unexpected empty time, however, can be a curse or a blessing. If we have nothing to do, we may fight our stomach anxiety as we hear the clock tick away. If we are prepared to do something, these tidbits can be a gift.

Gifts of time are encountered in a wide variety of ways: you have a scheduled meeting, but the other person is late; or you have to sit in the reception area much longer than expected; or on a field trip you find a whole afternoon free because some meetings were canceled, or an airline "equipment problem" means you have three hours to kill in an airport.

As one company president explains: "You don't have to talk to anybody on a plane, or at an airport. A couple of hours and you can do a tremendous amount of concentration, and that's impossible in the office."

These gifts of time can be used if you are prepared with material to work with. Thus, one of the most effective time utilizers I've ever seen always carries a briefcase containing three kinds of folders.

- manila folders containing current, responsive type items such as letters to be answered, production data to be checked, a rough draft of a report to be proofread and approved
- pink folders containing discretionary projects currently being worked on. These might include: tentative budget for next year, a new policy on individual performance evaluation, industry journals on a new technical development
- blue folders for notes on future, "blue sky" possibilities. When a bright idea strikes, it is written down and filed in a blue folder. Many of the ideas are "what if" questions: What would happen if we introduced a new product or revised an existing policy?

If the manager is feeling in peak form, he or she may peruse the ideas collected in the blue folders and decide which ones are promising enough to be transferred to the pink folders and converted into current discretionary projects, or may push ahead on the current pink folders.

If the unexpected time tidbit is of short duration or if the manager is feeling somewhat tired, he or she will focus on the manila folders, processing the fairly routine response type items.

Clark Kerr, the renowned labor relations scholar and former president of the University of California, was once asked how he managed to publish so many papers even while heading the nation's largest university. He replied that he did all of his writing in airport waiting rooms. The key in utilizing such bits of time is to control your anger at losing time and be physically prepared with working materials (it may also help to have a large briefcase and a strong arm!).

Exercise Two

DISTINGUISHING URGENCY FROM IMPORTANCE

OBJECTIVES

- to analyze the major activities in your job for urgency and importance
- to recognize that your most important activities tend not to be urgent—and that your most urgent-appearing tasks are usually not the most important

Reprinted by permission: Tribune Media Services

A. EXERCISE—LISTING YOUR ACTIVITIES

List all of the recurring activities that comprise your job. Don't list them in order of priority, but according to some schema that ensures that your list is comprehensive. Include routine matters and predictable emergencies. The list should take no more than 30 minutes to complete and should fit on this page.

_____

_____

_____

_____

_____

_____

_____

_____

_____

_____

_____

_____

_____

_____

_____

_____

_____

_____

_____

_____

_____

B. URGENCY ANALYSIS

Make a copy of your list of activities. Scissor the entries apart and distribute them among the four categories below.

---

1. Very Urgent: must be done immediately after the cue or at the scheduled time

---

---

2. Urgent: should be done within hours of the cue

---

3. Not Urgent: can be done in next few days or weeks

---

4. Time Not a Factor: might be done over few months or year

C. IMPORTANCE ANALYSIS

Make another copy of your activities list. Once again parcel the entries across the categories below, this time on the basis of intrinsic importance to you and your organization.

1. Very Important: must be done

_____

_____

_____

_____

_____

_____

2. Important: should be done

_____

_____

_____

_____

_____

_____

_____

_____

3. Not so Important: would be useful, but not essential

_____

_____

_____

_____

_____

_____

4. Unimportant: might be eliminated

_____

_____

_____

_____

D. DISCUSSION—ANALYZING YOUR ACTIVITIES TO DISTINGUISH THE URGENT FROM THE IMPORTANT

Effective time managers are aware of the difference between urgency and importance. They recognize that their most important duties are often not urgent in the sense that they must be done immediately after some cue. Your most important objectives tend to be only ambiguously or internally cued so that you must fight for time to allocate to them lest you be swallowed up by the explicitly cued but less important urgent items.

Exhibit 2-1 illustrates my activities as a university vice president supervising a department of 120 people responsible for alumni relations, public relations, publications, and fund raising. I listed my activities according to the people involved, starting with the president, then outside alumni, corporations and foundations, followed by various insiders including deans, peer executives, subordinates, and finally, trustees.

Exhibit 2-2 illustrates my urgency analysis, which shows how "very urgent" activities include attendance at meetings that the president or trustees schedule at their convenience (rather than mine). I must attend at the time cued on the calendar or miss the meeting. My "urgent" list

EXHIBIT 2.1: Activity Analysis—List of Activities for Vice President of Development and University Relations

- propose/advise president on his personal cultivation and solicitations
- participate in president's senior management group meetings
- participate in president's administrative staff meetings
- support president/attend university-wide events
- prepare, argue for, and negotiate about annual departmental budget
- call on/develop new individual alumni relationships
- solicit gifts from (a) alumni, (b) friends, (c) corporations, and (d) foundations
- respond to individual alumni calls/complaints about admissions, gifts
- initiate letters to alumni about their public accomplishments
- monitor gift receipts and acknowledgment letters
- maintain relations with deans of schools
- solve personnel and gift situation problems with deans
- recruit and hire senior development and public relations staff
- deal with university human resources office on salary and job classification situations
- plan strategy and design organization structure for (a) development, (b) university relations, and (c) alumni relations
- meet with senior departmental staff as individuals and in groups
- respond to senior departmental staff requests and inquiries
- conduct annual performance reviews with senior staff
- review and make salary decisions on all professional staff
- serve as cheerleader/maintain morale for staff through visits and entertainments
- meet with/advise alumni job seekers
- attend professional association meetings
- maintain relations with other university department senior managers
- serve as liaison to Trustee Development and University Relations Committees
- prepare agenda and make reports to two Trustee Committees
- maintain relations with Trustee chairpersons and members
- maintain relations with Alumni Regional Development Committees

EXHIBIT 2.2:   Activity Analysis for Urgency for Vice President of Development and
                   University Relations

Very Urgent (must be done immediately after cue or at scheduled time)

- propose/advise president on his personal cultivation and solicitations
- participate in president's senior management group meetings
- participate in president's administrative staff meetings
- support president/attend university-wide events
- support schools/attend Overseer meetings and events
- serve as liaison to Trustee Development and University Relations Committees

Urgent (should be done within hours after cue)

- monitor gift receipts and acknowledgement letters
- solve personnel and gift situation problems and deans
- recruit and hire senior development and public relations staff
- deal with university human resources office on salary and job classification
  situations
- meet with senior departmental staff as individuals and in group
- respond to senior departmental staff requests and inquiries
- conduct annual performance reviews with senior staff
- review and make salary decisions on all professional staff
- serve as cheerleader/maintain morale for staff through visits and entertainments
- meet with/advise alumni job seekers
- attend professional association meetings
- maintain relations with other university department senior managers
- prepare agenda and make reports to two Trustee Committees

Not Urgent (can be done during the four-month semester)

- prepare, argue for, and negotiate about annual departmental budget
- call on/develop new individual alumni relationships
- attend regional alumni relations meetings
- solicit gifts from (a) alumni, (b) friends, (c) corporations, and (d) individuals
- respond to individual alumni calls/complaints about admissions, gifts
- make decisions on alumni children applications to support
- initiate letters to alumni about their public accomplishments
- maintain relationships with deans of schools
- plan strategy and design organization structure for (a) development, (b) university
  relations, and (c) alumni relations
- maintain relations with Trustee chairpersons and members
- maintain relations with Alumni Regional Development Committee

Not Urgent: long range

- in fund raising, public relations, and alumni communications, explore ways of
  emphasizing the central and the whole
- propose means of generating development investment funds beyond the president's
  budget allocation
- find ways of providing performance-based rewards such as bonuses for outstanding
  individual or unit performance

is somewhat longer than the very urgent because I felt on most matters that I had from three to eight hours to deal with the issue or at least get back to the relevant person before the end of the day.

The third category in Exhibit 2-2, "not urgent," is comprised of activities and projects that I envisioned dealing with over a four-month semester. On most of these I enjoyed discretionary control over when I performed the activities. The very short list under "time not a factor" reflects those major long-range projects that I hoped to accomplish over several years (the paucity of this list may well reflect my tendency to be submerged in the short run).

Activity analysis for importance is a bit more difficult than for urgency. "Intrinsic importance" is a subjective concept that might reflect several questions:

- What activities have the most moral legitimacy given the mission of your institution?
- What activities, if done well, could lead to your being rewarded and honored by the institution (my predecessor had a building named after him)?
- What activities, if done poorly, would likely result in your being asked to resign (or get you fired in a less polite organization)?
- What activities if not performed would not be missed by anyone who could hurt (or help) you?

Exhibit 2-3 indicates my activity analysis for intrinsic importance. At the top of my "very important" category is proposing/advising the president on his personal cultivation and solicitation. This was extremely important because my school had just changed presidents and the former incumbent had not been an effective fund raiser. I thought it critical that the new president get involved in the activity in a way that he would find enjoyable and would allow him to be effective. My own cultivation and solicitation are third and fourth on the importance list.

Second in importance was my effort to improve the annual development and university relations budget. Since budget strategy had drifted in the past, I felt it imperative that a fresh approach be developed and that argument in its favor be energetic and persuasive.

Next on the list was dealing with admission applications of certain alumni children. Nothing quite touches an alumnus/alumna's emotions like having a child rejected, especially if the decision appears to be unfeelingly bureaucratic. Graciously handling applications from children of all, but especially influential and potentially helpful alumni, is of great importance.

After working closely with the deans of my university's 12 schools came effective representation to the central human resources office of the need for appropriate salaries and job classifications. Like many central salary administration units, ours found it difficult to keep up with a competitive labor market where experienced development professionals were in such demand that salaries were rising faster than the university personnel office wanted to admit.

EXHIBIT 2.3: Activity Analysis for Intrinsic Importance for Vice President for Development and University Relations

Very Important: must be done

- propose/advise president on his personal cultivation and solicitations
- prepare, argue for, and negotiate about annual departmental budget
- call on/develop new individual alumni relationships
- solicit gifts from (a) alumni, (b) friends, (c) corporations, and (d) individuals
- make decisions on alumni children applications to support
- solve personnel and gift situation problems with deans
- recruit and hire senior development and public relations staff
- deal with university human resources office on salary and job classification situations
- plan strategy and design organization structure for (a) development, (b) university relations, and (c) alumni relations
- review and make salary decisions on all professional staff
- serve as liaison to Trustee Development and University Relations Committee
- prepare agenda and make reports to two Trustee Committees

Important: should be done

- participate in president's senior management group meetings
- respond to individual alumni calls/complaints about admissions, gifts
- maintain relationships with deans of schools
- meet with senior departmental staff as individuals and in group
- respond to senior departmental staff requests and inquiries
- serve as cheerleader/maintain morale for staff through visits and entertainments
- maintain relations with Trustee chairpersons and members
- in fund raising, public relations, and alumni communications, explore ways of emphasizing the central and the whole
- propose means of generating development investment funds beyond the president's budget allocation
- find ways of providing performance-based rewards such as bonuses for outstanding individual or unit performance

Not So Important (not necessary, but useful)

- participate in president's administrative staff meetings
- support president/attend university-wide events
- attend regional alumni relations meetings
- initiate letters to alumni about their public accomplishments
- monitor gift receipts and acknowledgment letters
- support schools/attend Overseer meetings and events
- conduct annual performance reviews with senior staff
- meet with/advise alumni job seekers
- attend professional association meetings
- maintain relations with other university department senior managers
- maintain relations with Alumni Regional Development Committees

Unimportant (can be eliminated)

- nothing!

Internal department planning and organizational structuring comes next along with performance reviews and salary increase decisions. Last on the very important category is serving as liaison to the trustee committees.

The "important—should be done" entries are judged to be somewhat less critical but clearly things that must be done in contrast to the third category, "not so important (not essential, but useful)." I unfortunately couldn't find anything to allocate to the last category of "unimportant—can be eliminated"—a difficulty that I'm sure most readers will share.

Now compare your urgency analysis and importance analysis pages. There should be few activities in the top categories of both analyses. That is, few activities will be "very important" *and* "very urgent." For the most part, important activities will not be urgent because they don't have to be performed immediately on cue. This distinction can be useful when we consider delegation analysis in Exercise Four.

ON WHEN ONCE
IS ENOUGH OR NOT ENOUGH
SINGLE VERSUS MULTIPLE HANDLING
IN MANAGEMENT

© 1976 by Sidney Harris, the Wall Street Journal.

Once is usually sufficient. Much time is wasted through unnecessary multiple handling of memos, letters, and reports. They flow on to a manager's desk; perhaps he or she scans them and allocates them to particular categories based on priority or topic. The pieces of paper are placed in the appropriate "pending" box or pigeonhole. Later, the manager pulls out one pile and rereads the material preparatory to dictating a rough draft reply. When typed, the rough draft is checked and revisions written on it. Finally, the finished draft is read and signed.

According to this scenario, a single paper may be handled four times. Much of this is unnecessary, wasteful, and actually an excuse for procrastination.

Saving Time Through Single Handling: If you attempt to maximize the number of items you handle only once, multiple consideration can be reduced. Of course you cannot and should not make immediate decisions on all issues, but the proportion can be enlarged.

Discipline is required and a personal expectation of handling most papers only once. It is a matter of attitude. The attitude, however, is facilitated by certain techniques.

Write on the original. Many letters can be answered by simply writing directly on the original. Return the original with your comments and keep a photocopy. Typing all interorganizational correspondence on printed company letterheads may be an expensive vanity. If your handwriting is illegible, keep a typewriter beside your desk and use it for short notes stapled to the original. Or precoded forms can be used to respond to routine inquiries. The appropriate communication can be checked.

Minimize dictation. Dictation is often used to postpone final decisions. You, the manager, dictate a tentative reply onto a tape knowing that it will be some time before the typed version is returned from the word processing group (e.g., typing pool). You know that you will be able to veto or revise an earlier position, perhaps even dictate an entirely new report.

But this can go on and on. The advantage of typing a rough draft yourself is that it seems more "real" than words on a tape. You can immediately see what it will look like in final draft. Perhaps you can simply send it via electronic mail or order it typed in final, authorizing word processing to sign your name. Thus, multiple handling is reduced.

Don't abuse your briefcase. Putting items into your briefcase to deal with later at home is a legitimate tactic. The problem is that we are not always honest with ourselves and others. Sometimes what goes into the briefcase are those matters we dislike handling or are unable to make a decision on during the day. They may not really be important, just unpleasant.

Worse, the bulging briefcase can reflect a martyr complex. We want others and especially family to see how hard we are overworked. In a perverse way, taking work home convinces us that we are really important.

Worst of all, the briefcase can be used to manipulate our families. If they exert undesired demands on us to fix this broken appliance or play this juvenile game, with a long face we can point to the tyrannizing briefcase and complain that "I'd like to, but I can't." We may not even be aware of the deceit we thus practice on ourselves and others. Miraculously, the insistent demands of the briefcase papers can evaporate when we suggest a movie or game we would like to see!

When Multiple Handling is Desirable: Risk is involved in single handling. Mistakes are missed that might have been detected by multiple readings. Decisiveness is not always a virtue.

The renowned wit, author, and entertainer Gypsy Rose Lee once observed, "Anything that is worth doing well, is worth doing slowly." Certain matters should be handled slowly. Decisions regarding hiring, firing, promoting, transferring, and evaluating should allow for plenty of experiential data to be gathered. Such personnel decisions should go slowly, because they have long-lasting effects and are predominantly one-way. It is much easier to hire than fire, to promote than demote, and to assign than relieve.

That decision slowness can be desirable was sharply brought to my attention when I first started my research in the U.S. Senate. A senate leader hoped I was not an "efficiency expert" trying to make the Senate more efficient. He argued that the Senate is not supposed to be efficient, that bills should travel slowly, thus providing time for close examination, weakness correction, and democracy to work its will (one could counterargue, however, that three years to write an energy bill is a trifle long!).

A pharmaceutical company executive explains that virtually all pieces of paper must be handled multiple times to reduce error. Because of the seriousness of mistakes and the firm's legal vulnerability, multiple reading by different people is valid. Time consuming it is, but not necessarily wasteful.

But multiple handling must justify itself; it should not be mere habit or an excuse for procrastination.

Exercise Three

EMPHASIZING
WHERE YOU MAKE
THE GREATEST DIFFERENCE

OBJECTIVES

- to compare your performance on job tasks with those to whom they might be delegated
- to determine the activities on which you enjoy the greatest differential advantage

A. EXERCISE—ANALYZING DIFFERENTIAL ADVANTAGE

Working from your importance analysis in the previous exercise, subjectively rate your personal performance on each of your very important and important activities in comparison with those to whom the task might be delegated.

	Performance									
	1	2	3	4	5	6	7	8	9	10
	poor				satisfactory					exceptional
Activity										
me										
?										
me										
?										
me										
?										
me										
?										
me										
?										
me										
?										
me										
?										
me										
?										

Activity		1 poor	2	3	4	Performance 5 satisfactory	6	7	8	9	10 exceptional
	me										
	?										
	me										
	?										
	me										
	?										
	me										
	?										
	me										
	?										
	me										
	?										
	me										
	?										
	me										
	?										

B. DISCUSSION—FOCUS ON WHERE YOU HAVE THE GREATEST ADVANTAGE

A manager has an obligation to optimize the performance of the unit he or she directs. You should not allow your time to be consumed by the activities you most enjoy, or even those you do best. Rather, you should focus on those activities on which you enjoy the greatest differential advantage over those to whom they might be delegated.

One of the criticisms of Jimmy Carter as President of the United States was his apparent immersion in details to the detriment of communicating the big picture to the American public—and particularly to Congress. Extremely bright and more technologically literate than any prior president (except perhaps Herbert Hoover), he focused a major portion of his time on analyzing problems and formulating detailed legislation to be proposed to Capitol Hill. However, he delegated the actual lobbying for those bills to junior aids who shared his skepticism about senators and representatives. Standing on the White House balcony with President Bush recently, long-time Democratic party leader Robert Strauss recalled his 1977 advice to Carter:

> I told him to invite (Senators) Russell Long and Bob Dole up here and have a drink out on this wonderful balcony and then go and have dinner. . . . When it's all over, sometime during the evening, Russell Long will tell you how to get your tax bill done.

Unfortunately, President Carter didn't take the advice. Because he had run for president as an outsider and because he simply didn't enjoy schmoozing with legislators, he never developed the personal relationships essential to getting his proposals implemented. There is an old saying in Washington, DC that "no one gives a damn about having breakfast with the vice president." This is not a comment on any particular vice president; it simply reflects the fact that the president's differential advantage over the vice-president or any White House staffer is so great that his time must be focused on those activities where he (or she someday) can make the biggest difference.

Ronald Reagan understood this, especially early in his administration. The day after his November 1980 election, he visited on Capitol Hill. Four times before his first inauguration, he held meetings with Congressional leaders in their offices. In his first six months as president, he held over one hundred one-on-one meetings with senators and representatives—a multiple of what Carter did in four years. All of this contributed to President Reagan's greater success in seeing his proposals implemented into law (whatever one may feel about the substance of some of that legislation).

Focusing according to any criterion entails risk. It means being less knowledgeable of activities that you are not doing personally (and all presidents, but especially Reagan, have suffered for this). But this is one of the burdens of being a manager that must be borne if one is to have effective opportunity to make good things happen through one's personal attention.

You should compare your own performance on your important activities with that of the best available subordinate. You may even be a genius who does every activity better than any of your subordinates. But your superiority will vary by task. Task A, for example, may be something you do extremely well; you enjoy the sense of accomplishment as it feeds your need for achievement. You rate yourself a 9. But your subordinate Amy can perform the task almost as well (at 7) so your advantage is small—only $9 - 7 = 2$. Task B, however, is something you don't do as well as A (and perhaps don't enjoy as much). Unfortunately, Bob is the only possible delegatee and his performance is markedly below yours—

EXHIBIT 3.1:   Sample Differential Advantage Analysis for Vice President for Development and University Relations

		Performance										
		1	2	3	4	5	6	7	8	9	10	
		poor				satisfactory					exceptional	
Activity												
cultivate	**me**								8			+3
indiv alums	**Bill**					5						
solicit	**me**							7				−1
corps/fnds	**Cynthia**								8			
prepare/neg	**me**							7				+4
dept budget	**Maxine**			3								
write congrats	**me**									9		+1
to alumns	**Sam**								8			
liaison to	**me**									9		+1
Trustees	**Ed**								8			
monitor	**me**							7				−1
gift recpts	**Norma**								8			
deal with	**me**							7				+4
HR dept.	**Maxine**			3								
advise alum	**me**								8			0
job seekers	**Frank**								8			
respond to	**me**								8			+2
major donors	**Norma**					6						

a 2 compared with your 6. Assuming tasks A and B are equally important, you should focus on B since your differential advantage there is 4 compared with 2 on task A.

Exhibit 3-1 illustrates my application of this differential advantage analysis. Two activities on the list particularly illustrate this principle. Writing congratulatory letters to alumni was an activity that I enjoyed very much and did well. I was usually able to deliver a mix of institutional admiration with a gentle needle that *alma mater* missed their interest and financial support. Completing these letters gave me great satisfaction. But I had a full-time writing staff of four headed by a former business editor of a prominent newspaper. Although his writing was not as subtle as mine, my differential advantage was very small. Obviously this was not something on which I should expend my limited time.

Also, notice my comparison of performance on cultivating and soliciting gifts from individuals as compared with corporations and foundations. My differential advantage over my staff in calling on individuals was large. Because I was the only member of the staff with a background as a business school professor, because I was the only one with a vice president title (universities are loath to hand out such titles), and perhaps because of my personality, I enjoyed a substantial differential advantage on cultivating and soliciting individual alumni. With corporations and foundations, however, I had no advantage—and perhaps even a disadvantage. Corporate and foundation giving is a highly professionalized and bureaucratized activity with middle-level staffers at those institutions prescribing and processing specific forms from which they make recommendations that higher executives generally ratify. I had professional staff in corporate and foundation relations who knew these procedures and the people involved. My excessive and premature entry into the process might only screw it up. So my golden tongue might be saved only for a final touching base with senior executives of the donating firm rather than in the application stage.

Either through explicit analysis or intuitive insight, the most effective strategic time managers have a sense of where their personal attention and involvement will make the biggest difference in their organization's success.

ON BEING
OUT TO LUNCH
INSULATION AND ISOLATION
AS MANAGEMENT TACTICS

Drawing by Krahn: © 1963 The New Yorker Magazine Inc. Reprinted by permission.

Managers cannot control all of their time. Most of the time, they should be available to respond to other's questions, requests, and problems. Nonetheless, if managers allow such responses to eat up all their time, they will be tyrannized by the present. Life will be consumed fighting fires with no opportunity to prevent them.

Insulation and isolation are two techniques used to periodically escape in order to think about the longer term perspective.

Insulation: Managers can be buffered from organizational demands for limited time periods. The most common device is by scanning and sorting incoming communications. The classic illustration is the U.S. presidency. By executive order in 1939, Franklin D. Roosevelt created the Executive Office of the President "to protect the President's time" by "excluding any matter that can be settled elsewhere." This mechanism evolved into assistants who stand between the president and almost all incoming communications. They decide: (1) what matters should be brought to the president's attention, (2) by whom (the originator or by a White House aide), (3) how (by written or verbal communication), and (4) when.

In addition to controlling incoming communications, these assistants can also group conferences to specific periods that the Chief Executive prefers. Such grouping simplifies the president's preparation by concentrating overlapping areas.

Of course, most managers do not have such elaborate staffs. They must depend on an assistant—a secretary who does more than type and answer the phone. A competent buffer should have enough discretion to redirect about half of a manager's incoming messages to more appropriate people on matters that should reach the manager; an astute subordinate can save time by gathering relevant data and preparing preliminary suggestions. The intent is to ensure that the manager reads each incoming communication only once before a reply is drafted.

Isolation: One of the problems of open landscape office design has been the inability to insulate oneself. Managers appear always available because no buffering doors or walls exist, and therefore, private offices are coveted. Across the alley from the White House in the Executive Office Building, President Nixon had a small private office where he could work alone. All presidents have found it essential to have secluded retreats, as in Hyde Park, Key West, and Camp David. Business executives may also maintain two offices. An entrepreneur in Fairfield County, Connecticut, erected an office building specifically intended to provide second offices for Manhattan executives residing in Connecticut. As another alternative, some are able to work at home one day every week or two.

Danger in Insulation and Isolation: Periodic withdrawal seems so simple, but risks are involved. Can the manager afford to be unreachable? The President of the United States clearly cannot, so he has extensive communications equipment travel with him. Many managers take much the same view of themselves. If they are accessible, however, how can they confine interruptions only to true emergencies? Who makes this determination?

Excessive buffering of the U.S. president has been criticized as dangerous. The assistants may insulate the president from information they consider trivial, but which may really be important. The information reaching the executive may be so filtered and biased that he is out of touch with reality. The late Hubert Humphrey commented that he never perceived the magnitude of anti-Vietnam War feeling until he left the vice presidency. And former White House Press Secretary George Reedy argued that the problem of keeping a Chief Executive in touch with reality is so severe that it poses a danger to the future of our country. Reedy maintained that the White House is enveloped in a "velvet cocoon."

Any withdrawal may create personal animosity. The associate or subordinate who calls with a matter that is important to him or her may be offended when denied entry. Even tougher, courage is required to withdraw from a superior's initiations for *any* length of time. He or she may expect a subordinate to be always on tap.

In addition, the culture of the institution may discourage periodic withdrawal. At a meeting of church officials, one bishop maintained that withdrawal was simply impossible. The human values implicit in his religion's mission so permeate church administration that the administrator is expected to be shepherd and servant to his associates and subordinates. The value system requires that he be available, understanding, and responsive. Understandable as this is, it probably hurts the institution's effectiveness, because immediate problems will tend to dominate. Some periodical insulation is important for all managers.

Exercise Four

DELEGATING WHAT CAN BE DELEGATED

OBJECTIVES

- to decide what must be done and by you
- to experiment with what you might do a bit less conscientiously
- to determine what could be delegated

TANK McNAMARA, © 1989 UNIVERSAL PRESS SYNDICATE. Reprinted with permission. All rights reserved.

A. EXERCISE—ANALYZING ACTIVITIES FOR DELEGATION POTENTIAL

Drawing on Exercises 2 and 3, activity and differential advantage analysis, distribute your job activities among the three categories below.

Must Be Done and Must be Done by Me

_____

_____

_____

_____

_____

_____

_____

If Done Must Be Done by Me, But Relax (they don't always have to be done)

_____

_____

_____

_____

_____

_____

_____

Can be Delegated

_____

_____

_____

_____

_____

_____

_____

B. DISCUSSION—DELEGATION GUIDELINES

Activity and differential advantage analysis suggests some delegation guidelines. In general:

Keep for yourself:

- the relatively few (hopefully) very important *and* very urgent activities
- the very important but not urgent
- the important activities on which you enjoy the greatest differential advantage

Delegate:

- the important activities on which you have the smallest differential advantage (or a disadvantage)
- the urgent but not so important
- the unimportant (if do at all)

Exhibit 4-1 illustrates my own delegation analysis. The first category of "Must be done and must be done by me" reflects my judgment of importance and differential advantage. These are activities that simply must be done if the department is to succeed (and I was to survive). And these are activities where either because of my personal attributes or the clout of my office my differential advantage was greatest.

As a new vice president replacing a long-term incumbent, I felt it critical that I get control of the department budget and that the budget be significantly increased. It lagged in growth behind other university areas and was sharply below the fund-raising aspirations of a new president. It was my judgment that I was the best person to make this argument to the campus community.

Calling on alumni/alumnae, developing individual relationships, and soliciting gifts had to be more widely dispersed than the rather centralized manner in which it had been handled by my predecessor. Nonetheless, the development vice president at my institution had to be heavily involved personally in this activity. My aim was for a third of my time to be so allocated, but it was difficult getting it above 25 percent.

Personally working with all 12 deans was simply impossible, so I focused my personal involvement on the four schools judged most central to the university's academic mission and most important for fund-raising potential (unfortunately, the two dimensions didn't correspond—and don't ask what schools they were!). Of course, I didn't make a public announcement of my distinction, but set up a system for my key aids to become the primary liaisons with the deans of the other eight schools.

As mentioned earlier, competition for good development professionals has become severe. Both because of my status as vice president and my interpersonal skills, I deemed it imperative that I devote substantial personal time to this process, even to the hiring of people several levels down in the hierarchy. And if these people were to be attracted and retained, their job classifications and salaries had to reflect market reality. Therefore, I had to represent this need to a sometimes reluctant university human resources department.

EXHIBIT 4-1: Activity Analysis for Delegation for Vice President for Development and University Relations

---

Must Be Done By Me

- prepare, argue for, and negotiate about annual departmental budget
- call on/develop new individual alumni relationships
- solicit gifts from (a) alumni, (b) friends
- make decisions on alumni children applications to support
- maintain relationships with deans of schools—major schools only
- solve personnel and gift situation problems with deans
- recruit and hire senior development and public relations staff
- deal with university human resources office on salary and job classification situations
- plan strategy and design organization structure for (a) development, (b) university relations, and (c) alumni relations
- meet with senior departmental staff as individuals and in group
- respond to senior departmental staff requests and inquiries
- review and make salary decisions on all professional staff
- serve as cheerleader/maintain morale for staff through visits and entertainments
- propose means of generating development investment funds beyond the president's budget allocation
- find ways of providing performance-based rewards such as bonuses for outstanding individual or unit performance

---

Must be Done by Me, but Relax (don't be so conscientious)

- propose/advise president on his personal cultivation and solicitations
- participate in president's Senior Management Group meetings
- participate in president's administrative staff meetings
- support president/attend university-wide events
- attend regional alumni relations meetings
- support schools/attend Overseer meetings and events
- conduct annual performance reviews with senior staff
- attend professional association meetings
- maintain relations with other university department senior managers

---

Can be Delegated

- solicit gifts from (c) corporations and (d) foundations
- respond to individual alumni calls/complaints about admissions, gifts
- initiate letters to alumni about their public accomplishments
- monitor gift receipts and acknowledgment letters
- maintain relations with deans (minor schools)
- meet with/advise alumni job seekers
- serve as liaison to Trustee Development and University Relations Committees
- prepare agenda and make reports to two trustee committees
- maintain relations with chairpersons and members
- maintain relations with Alumni Regional Development Committees
- in fund raising, public relations, and alumni communications, explore ways of emphasizing the central and the whole

---

The other entries in this category of "Must be done and must be done by me" are self-explanatory and reflect administrative process and ritual that a senior manager must handle personally.

The second category, "Must be done by me, but relax," is a "don't be so conscientious" category. The activities can't be delegated entirely, but some proportion of the cues could be ignored and the activities not always performed. My analysis in Exhibit 4-1 in this category contains mostly standing meetings and ritualistic events. The first entry "propose/advise president on his personal cultivation and solicitations" is obviously extremely important—perhaps the most important responsibility that I had. Nonetheless, I discovered that as his confidence in my director of development (and other staff) grew, it was not necessary for me to attend every one of these meetings. It appears that if I made two-thirds of them, I could safely miss the others in order to be on the road for my own cultivations and solicitations.

Similarly, the second entry on participating in the president's senior management meetings is extremely important, for this is the highest policy group in the university. It was a great opportunity for development and university relations to be represented at this level, along with the provost as chief academic officer, the executive director of the budget, the senior vice president for business affairs, and the vice president for medical affairs. But the weekly meetings were on Wednesdays and I could safely miss about a quarter of them in order to take longer trips.

Participation in the larger president's administrative staff (about 30 people) and attending university-wide ceremonies were situations where there was substantial tolerance for my need to be elsewhere (although I had to fight my own guilt feelings every time).

Being less conscientious in attending regional alumni relations meetings was difficult for me because I valued these events and enjoyed making contacts with large numbers of alumni. But the somewhat harsh reality that I came to recognize is that these meetings were not essential for my more important fund-raising activity. Alumni/ae with the means to make large individual gifts rarely attend such group events—and even if some do, the contact quality is markedly inferior to a visit in the office or home. Therefore, attendance at alumni receptions was fitted into cultivation/solicitation travel and made subordinate to it.

Attendance at individual school events was reduced by giving major attention to the four critical schools and assigning representatives for most other events—although it was very difficult to avoid attending a school overseer meeting when invited because these groups usually contained some trustees and significant donors.

Over time, I somewhat reduced the time devoted to formal performance reviews with my senior staff. Our communications improved and performance feedback occurred more frequently and more informally. In addition, however, I increasingly came to feel that the formal performance review system was not effective because it was not linked to salary increases and I was blocked by university salary policy from giving bonuses.

The remaining activities are those that I concluded could be delegated most, if not all, the time. In general, these are activities on which I enjoyed little differential advantage—and some where subordinates could do a markedly better job than I.

In general, both less effective *and* more effective time managers do what must be done. The more effective, however, are more assertive in delegating and more experimental in selectively ignoring certain activities.

ON THE CONFUSION OF "EITHER . . . OR:" GUIDELINES FOR CLARIFYING DELEGATION

Drawing by Day; © The New Yorker Magazine, Inc. Reprinted by permission.

Delegation is not "either I do it, or you do it." Rather, delegating comes in several forms. Ambiguity about them is one of the biggest time wasters in modern organizations.

Many of today's executives were exposed years ago in primary school to a homily entitled "A Message to Garcia." During the Spanish-American War 90 years ago, a young Army lieutenant was called to the White House and directed to carry a letter to a guerilla leader named Garcia who was fighting the Spanish in the Cuban mountains. The Army officer in effect saluted, said "yes, sir," and departed. He asked no questions about how he was to go, who would pay for transportation, if he would be paid for overtime, and so on. No complaints were voiced about how it would interfere with his skiing weekend or that he disliked hot weather.

The pamphlet on Garcia was distributed to thousands of school children as a lesson in obedience, a model of proper subordinate behavior. The tale's moral has some validity. A superior has a right to expect obedience if his or her directives are legitimate. And most of us admire subordinate self-reliance.

Nonetheless, the story is more wrong than right. Aside from the moral dangers in blindly following orders, such behavior can waste huge gobs of time. A subordinate is given an order. Thinking he understands, he accepts the obligation and charges off. But when the task is completed, all too often a disappointed superior realizes that the wrong job was performed because the subordinate didn't understand what was desired.

A recurring problem is that the harried superior doesn't take time to define what is expected and an inexperienced or fearful subordinate doesn't ask the tough questions necessary to clarify the situation. Both parties should recognize that there are several forms of delegation. And each should know what form is intended between them. For example, when a superior delegates to a subordinate, he or she should clarify what initiative is expected from the subordinate. But if the boss doesn't do so, a subordinate might ask one or more of the following questions:

1. After I look into this problem, should I give you all the facts so that you can decide what to do?
2. Should I let you know the alternatives available with the pros and cons of each so you can decide which to select?
3. Should I recommend a course of action for your approval?
4. Should I let you know what I intend to do, but delay action until you approve?
5. Should I let you know what I intend to do and do it unless you say not to?
6. Should I take action, let you know what I did, and inform you of the results?
7. Should I take action and communicate with you only if my action is unsuccessful?
8. Should I take action without additional communication with you?

Clarity in initial instructions will save time and embarrassment. After the pattern is defined, the superior should adhere to it consistently to the completion of the delegated task. Without such clarification and consistency, anxious subordinates may tend toward patterns 1 and 2 because they fear taking action for which they could be criticized. As a consequence, the superior will be continually consulted and possibly submerged in trivia.

Effective delegators strive to define their expectations clearly, but even more importantly, to invite a subordinate's clarifying questions.

Exercise Five

MAXIMIZING DELEGATION FREEDOM

OBJECTIVES

- to understand the forms of delegation along the delegation continuum
- to analyze how the degree of freedom in delegation can be increased

"Mr. Edwards, this is your secretary, Melissa. When you have a moment, would you run down and get me a regular coffee and a pineapple Danish?"

Drawing by Darrow: © The New Yorker Magazine, Inc. Reprinted by permission.

A. EXERCISE—ANALYSIS OF DELEGATION FORMS

Locate the major activities you feel you can delegate in the appropriate category along the continuum of delegation degree of freedom.

LEAST SUBORDINATE FREEDOM

1. Look into this problem; give me all the facts; I will decide what to do.

_____

_____

2. Let me know the alternatives with pros and cons; I will decide what to do.

_____

_____

3. Recommend a course of action for my approval.

_____

_____

4. Let me know what you intend to do; delay action until I ratify it.

_____

_____

5. Let me know what you intend to do; do it unless I say no.

_____

_____

6. Take action; let me know what you did and how it turns out.

_____

_____

7. Take action; communicate with me only if your action is unsuccessful.

_____

_____

8. Take action; no further communication with me is necessary.

_____

_____

MOST SUBORDINATE FREEDOM

B. DISCUSSION—DEGREES OF FREEDOM IN DELEGATION

The purpose of delegation is to transfer legitimate power from a superior to a subordinate so the latter can accomplish a necessary task. Unfortunately, so much delegation involves a begrudging assignment of tasks that managers would prefer to do themselves if only they had the time. And all time is not saved when a task is delegated. The superior must still supervise, monitor, and correct—especially inexperienced subordinates still learning their newly assigned tasks.

Some managers think they can do the job faster themselves. In the short run, they are probably correct. In the long run, however, delegation will enable the subordinates to develop competence and free superiors to devote time to other perhaps more important and challenging matters. That is, they will be freer if they have delegated clearly enough so that subordinates know what to do and what is expected. Unfortunately, a too frequently recurring problem is that harried superiors do not take the time to define what they expect, and inexperienced or fearful subordinates do not ask the tough questions to clarify what is expected.

Delegation lies upon a continuum. Both managers and subordinates should realize that multiple forms of delegation exist. And each group should know what form is intended between them—particularly what degree of initiative is expected of the subordinate. Consider the eight sets of instructions in Exhibit 5-1, which summarizes my own analysis.

When delegating, a manager should be clear about which of these patterns is intended. Clarity of initial instruction will save both time and embarrassment. After the pattern is defined, the superior should adhere to it consistently to the completion of the delegated task. Without such clarification and consistency, many subordinates will tend to patterns 1, 2, and 3 because they fear taking actions for which they will be criticized. More ambitious subordinates, however, may assume form 8 because it maximizes their freedom.

EXHIBIT 5-1: Delegation Degree of Freedom Analysis for Vice President for
Development and University Relations

**LEAST
SUBORDINATE
FREEDOM**

**MOST
SUBORDINATE
FREEDOM**

1. Look into this problem; give me all the facts; I will decide what to do.
- *gather information on budget expenditures and requests*

2. Let me know the alternatives with pros and cons; I will decide what to do.
- *recommend president's travel and donor solicitations*

3. Recommend a course of action for my approval.
- *Plan for alumni cultivation program*

4. Let me know what you intend to do; delay action until I ratify it.
- *prepare agenda for Trustees' meetings*

5. Let me know what you intend to do; do it unless I say no.
- *monitor individual gift receipts*
- *prepare thank you letters*

6. Take action; let me know what you did and how it turns out.
- *congratulatory letters on alum's accomplishments*
- *solicit gifts from corps and foundations*
- *maintain relations with deans of minor schools*

7. Take action; communicate with me only if your action is unsuccessful.
- *respond to individual alumni calls/complaints*
- *meet alumni job seekers*

8. Take action; no further communication with me is necessary.
- *plan and conduct regional alumni club meetings*

Note that no form of delegation is always better than any other. Each has its advantages and disadvantages. Consider some examples of U.S. presidents. Dwight Eisenhower was said to prefer delegation types 3 and 4. He wanted his White House assistants to provide a detailed proposal that he could approve and implement with his signature. This approach freed him from devoting time to detailed problem analysis and alternative generation. But it was precisely this aloofness that the incoming Kennedy administration in 1961 sharply criticized. John Kennedy favored delegation forms 1 and 2; he wanted to be involved in early discussion where his own intelligence and creativity could be applied (particularly after the 1961 Bay of Pigs fiasco where he felt he delegated excessive power to his military advisers). This may have worked for Kennedy (who was a speed reader) but it certainly consumes time and attention—which became especially evident in the stress that fell on President Jimmy Carter because of his apparent submergence in excessive detail.

Presidents Harry Truman and Ronald Reagan seemed to lean toward forms 7 and 8, which grant the greatest autonomy to subordinates and impose minimal time demands on the delegator. Indeed, Harry Truman was widely beloved by his subordinates for the enormous faith he expressed in them. One Cabinet member reported that he once tried to report to Truman on his activities, but the president cut him short: "John, you're doing a good job. You'll hear from me when you're not. Now, let's talk about the Civil War." In similar fashion, President Reagan was praised by subordinates and others for his broad delegation.

The problem with delegating in forms 7 and 8 is that the superior runs the risk of being out of touch with what is going on (*Fortune* magazine did a cover article in the summer of 1986 praising Reagan's ability to find good people, then to delegate tasks and leave them alone—just months before the Iran-Contra affair began to come to light). An organization's interest can be severely endangered by an out-of-control subordinate. Truman experienced this with the highly revered General Douglas MacArthur who, as supreme allied commander in the Far East during the Korean War, threatened to invade China (and perhaps use nuclear tactical weapons) without the authority of the president. Because he had such weak in-process control, Truman's options were reduced to only the exercise of his ultimate power to fire MacArthur from his job— at immense political cost to the president. Some would argue that Reagan confronted the same problem with his national security adviser John Poindexter and his assistant Oliver North.

Even with its risks, however, effective strategic time managers invest time in training their subordinates so they can safely push their delegation forms down the delegation continuum toward a greater degree of freedom, hence giving subordinates more autonomy and saving the managers' time.

ON SAYING "NO"
TO THE BOSS
A TACTIC
FOR HANDLING OVERLOAD

Drawing by Vietor; © The New Yorker Magazine, Inc. Reprinted by permission.

Yes? No? More? Less? Go? Stay? Now? Later? Slow? Quick? He? She? Black? White? Young? Old? New? Used? Lead? Lag? . . . Like Macbeth's battalions of troubles, a multitude of decisions press on managers—decisions that grow increasingly complex and time-consuming. And there's the rub; time does not grow with the expanding number, scope, and importance of these decisions. Indeed, it seems to shrink. And with that apparent shrinkage comes stress.

The Danger in Saying "yes":   The easiest but most dangerous tactic for handling role overload is to work longer, play less, and sleep little. Ambitious young people are particularly prone to say "yes" to all demands, hoping to make themselves indispensable. Unfortunately, this suits only Superman and Wonder Woman. Most of us simply can't meet all the demands on our time. To attempt to do so breeds physical and psychological disaster.

And simply saying yes is a passive response. You abdicate all control over your life. The paradox is that it may be the most promising young men and women who find it easiest to drift. To be in demand is a mark of status. Being busy conveys importance. But as so often happens to young accountants and consultants, they overcommit themselves, miss deadlines (that most heinous of organization crimes), lose credibility, and burn out. Ambitious young women may be even more subject to this danger because they want to appear strong and independent.

The Advantage of Saying "no":   Managers should learn how to say "no" to their superiors while encouraging subordinates to say "no" to them. Many superiors are horrified at the idea, but consider the point. A manager has a right to expect that his or her subordinates will generally do what they are told. Sometimes, however, a subordinate has an obligation not to do what a superior directs.

Newton Minow was President John Kennedy's Director of the Federal Communications Commission. One evening Kennedy became extremely angry after watching the Huntley-Brinkley news report. He felt they had unjustly criticized him. In a fit of rage, he called Minow on the telephone and with various colorful oaths ordered his aid to punish NBC, to "get" those S.O.B.s through any means available. Minow replied that he would look into it.

But Minow did nothing. The next day he wrote a note to Kennedy indicating how lucky the president was to have subordinates who were so loyal that they didn't always do what they were told. Kennedy recognized Minow's wisdom, and called him with thanks. Minow believed, and Kennedy agreed (when his anger had abated), that a loyal subordinate sometimes should say "no" in order to protect the boss from the consequences of his own folly.

Saying "no" extends to telling a superior when his or her time demands are excessive or deadlines impossible to meet. The word "no" is in quotes because it doesn't mean to refuse a task. Rather, subordinates should try to bargain with their superiors with respect to unreasonable demands. Don't passively accept a deadline when you know meeting it will be impossible. To remain silent will mislead the superior into thinking the job will be done on time.

The obligation of subordinates to sometimes say "no" to their superiors creates a mutual need to encourage your subordinates to sometimes say "no" to you. As a superior, you must not abdicate to your subordinates, but you should at least be receptive to their questioning of your time demands. You should be willing to bargain with your subordinates on these matters just as you sometimes want to negotiate with your superior.

All of this saying "no" and bargaining is easier said than done of course. Substantial courage and self-control may be required. An astute manager will battle to change role demands, but not always. No one can fight all the time, or his or her influence upward will be totally expended and credibility gone. Like an army general, this manager battles only on the most favorable grounds.

Exercise Six

REDUCING
ROLE OVERLOAD

OBJECTIVES

- to define the sources of your multiple role demands
- to analyze the demands
- to develop tactics for priority response, selective ignorance, and renegotiation

A. EXERCISE—PLOTTING THE DEMANDS ON YOU

Fill in the names of the people, organizations or institutions that make demands on you. Then analyze these demanders according to the following questions.

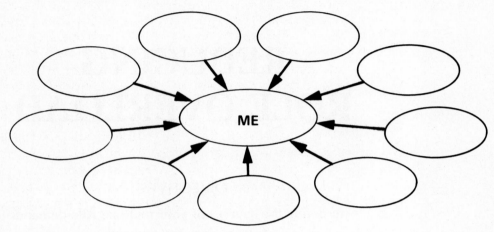

1. What demanders have the most power to help or hurt you?

_____

_____

_____

2. What demanders have the most right to make demands of you?

_____

_____

_____

3. What demanders could you ignore or withdraw from?

_____

_____

_____

4. What demands can be selectively ignored?

_____

_____

_____

5. What demands can be postponed until later in life?

_____

_____

_____

6. What demands can be negotiated?

_____

_____

_____

B. DISCUSSION—REDUCING ROLE OVERLOAD

Everybody in an organization is expected by his or her superiors, peers, subordinates, and others to behave in certain ways (called role demands). These demands are made by various people with whom we work and live (those role partners who collectively comprise one's role set). To all those in your role set, your effectiveness depends on how closely your behavior meets their demands. Your personal role satisfaction, however, depends on how closely your actual behavior fits your role desire. Very few of us are superpeople who can meet everyone's expectations and still be happy with our lives (if we are even able to survive!). Fortunately, some tactics exist for handling excessive demands.

Partial Withdrawal: Rather than fleeing to the South Seas from everyone and everything, you could ignore certain demanders, in effect withdrawing from (or postponing) some life dimensions. For example, ambitious young graduates frequently postpone marriage and family in order to simplify their lives while they focus on building a career. Ambitious family people, however, often ignore all requests from their communities to become involved in volunteer activities like coaching little league baseball, serving as a girl scout leader, or running for the school board. In older traditional families, husbands would simply abdicate all community relations to their homemaker spouses. In my own case, for 30 years my wife handled all communications with my parents, brothers, and sisters—Christmas presents, birthday cards, and birth congratulations. I'm not now proud of this, but it was certainly helpful to me. Now with over 50 percent of married women working outside the home, ignoring community expectations and needs has become even more common.

Selective Ignorance: Rather than withdrawing from a whole set of demanders like one's neighbors, you could instead accept some of their demands and reject others. Most students quickly size up a teacher to determine whether he or she *really* expects them to do all the reading as well as keep good class notes. Prior tests may suggest whether class or reading might be ignored. A college dormitory adviser might minimize communications with school administrators and quietly stop enforcing anti-drinking regulations while trying to remain an older sister and social leader with her residents. The university professor might simplify his situation by teaching as little as possible and hiding from students while focusing on his research and writing.

Rather than totally ignoring a person, you might compromise by responding only to exceptionally important demands. Thus, the competitive elements of conflicting demands might be reduced a bit. The dormitory adviser might take action only against *major* rule violations and ignore the more numerous minor ones (for example, ignoring underage drinking, but reporting illegal drugs). A newly promoted business supervisor might apply pressure on his former working buddies only when a crisis arises or when senior management is present. Otherwise, the supervisor adheres to the group's informal code and doesn't interfere with their horseplaying on the job.

Key in selective ignorance is accurate assessment of the political environment: just whose demands are more important or what expectations are less valid. Analyzing power and authority may be useful.

Respond to Power: The most pragmatic response to conflicting demands from various people is to minimize potential pain by giving priority to the person who can punish (or reward) you. Working parents, for example, tend to give priority to job demands at the expense of children and spouse. Only 6 percent of women and 7 percent of men say they slight their job to satisfy family demands, but 30 percent of women and 33 percent of men feel that children's demands are given lower priority when there is a conflict between a working parent's job and home. Children simply are deemed to have less power than employers.

When faced with dangerous role overload, it is certainly legitimate to examine what demanders can be ignored. One needs to be aware, however, that there are consequences. Ignored children, for example, often get an unintended revenge. The number one cause of guilt feelings among executives is not making a bad decision on the job; it is guilt about not paying enough attention to their children.

At work, the political question is who has the most power to satisfy or frustrate your needs. This is likely to be some hierarchical superior. Unfortunately, it is not always easy to determine who has the most power. And even if you know this, responding only to that person can still hurt you because ignored others may possess sufficient power to retaliate—and your preferred one may not want to expend political capital to defend you.

Even your boss may not be happy if giving him or her priority means your role is not performed well. Lower rated managers seem to conform the most to direct superiors, while higher rated managers ignore demands that interfere with performance. They get the job done, and most superiors value results over blind obedience.

Respond to Legitimacy: Rather than raw power, you could give priority to the demands judged most legitimate. The questions are: "Who has the most right to the results of my performance?" Or, "What behavior on my part will contribute most to the organization's mission?" Power and legitimacy may reside in the same superior, but not always. A powerful vice president might bypass your department head to direct you to concentrate on "Project Baker," while your direct superior wants "Project Able" completed first. The most legitimate demand is probably the department head's.

Compartmentalization of Responses: Under stress you can define arbitrary personal rules that separate demand responses. Usually this means changing priorities depending on where in the daily, weekly, monthly, or yearly calendar the demand occurs. For example, a professor might sequence demand response by devoting Tuesdays and Thursdays wholly to classes and students; Mondays to paperwork, committees, and administrative chores; Wednesdays to earning extra income through consulting; and Fridays and weekends to research and writing. Note that the intent of such arbitrary rules is to simplify the professor's life. She does not have to decide what to do with each demand; she just fits it into a category (so if a student knocks at her office door on a Friday when she is writing, the knock is ignored—not "fair" and not pretty, but effective).

Although business managers seldom enjoy the discretionary control over their time that professors do, an executive might allot three nights a week to his family regardless of job demands, but on other nights unexpected job demands have priority regardless of his daughter's field

hockey game or his wife's need for assistance with the laundry. The
advantage of such impersonal rules is that you don't have to analyze the
specific situation before applying the prescription. You don't have to
reinvent the wheel repeatedly.

Increasingly this approach is being applied to people's lives and
careers. Many young people are simply postponing family demands early
in their careers in order to give priority to job demands. They hope that
early success will give them political strength and financial resources later
to withdraw partially from the job and then better balance work and
personal demands. For some women, this takes the form of temporary
partial withdrawal after an early fast start in order to give more time to
family for a while before reassuming a larger commitment to career. Such
approaches can be wise, but they are not guaranteed to be successful
given the vagaries of humankind's biological clocks, the work and fun
of being a full-time parent, and a firm's uncertainty about the true commitment of someone who partially withdraws for a time.

Renegotiation of Demands: The most courageous response to role
stress is to modify the demands on you by confronting your role set. The
misassigned individual could apply for a transfer; the underchallenged
could request more interesting work (or just find it and *do it*); and the
overwhelmed could demand less pressure. Or a person suffering role
conflict could inform his or her superiors that they should coordinate
their demands. The college dormitory adviser could ask to be relieved
of her police duties; the professor could request evaluation as a teacher
or researcher, but not both; the supervisor could ask for a transfer to a
department where he is not supervising old friends; the division general
manager could ask central corporate staff to rescind undesired policies;
and spouses could agree to change their mutual expectations.

All of these initiatives involve small acts of courage because the
people imposing demands may be unwilling to modify them. Whether
their reasons for refusal are valid or not is quite irrelevant if they believe
in their legitimacy. A wife who talks with her spouse about changing
the ground rules over respective duties can deeply offend the other party.
An organizational superior might become angry with a star performing
woman who requests a reduction in her responsibilities for a period of
time so she can care for her young children. And if the subordinate
becomes too insistent, the boss may threaten retaliation.

A sense of proportion is critical. An astute manager will fight to
change role demands, but not always. A division general manager, for
example, should oppose the most crippling central policies, but continual
fighting can exhaust his upward influence and destroy credibility.

Exhibit 6-1 illustrates the role demand analysis for a U.S. senator
with whom I once worked. A relatively young man, he was ambitious
for the vice presidency, so he found it very difficult to ignore any of the
demands put upon him. He essentially structured his office to focus on
constituent letters and telephone calls, believing that acting as an "ombudsman" for his state's voters would secure his political position. This
meant that he personally and his staff focused on political "retailing"
and not "wholesaling" (if you remember the Senator Ribicoff example
from the introduction). Unfortunately, this orientation meant that very
little time was devoted to drafting and pushing legislation that dealt with

EXHIBIT 6-1:   Role Analysis for U.S. Senator

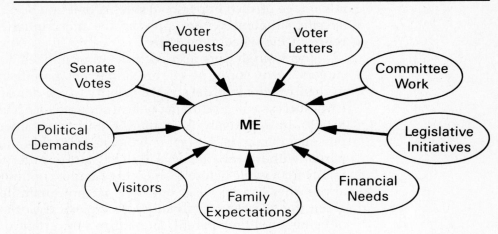

1. What demanders have the most power to help or hurt you?
- Voters
- Political allies & enemies
- Family

3. What demanders could you ignore or withdraw from?
Senate colleagues/Voters

Visitors

5. What demands can be postponed until later in life?
Legislative initiatives

Family expectations?

Financial needs?

2. What demanders have the most right to make demands of you?
- Voters
- Family
- Senate colleagues

4. What demands can be selectively ignored?
Legislative initiatives

Family expectations

Visitors

6. What demands can be negotiated?
Political demands

Family expectations

national problems. He didn't invest time in building Capitol Hill contacts and developed little clout with his colleagues (in spite of his popularity with his home state voters). His life was so rooted in immediate tasks that after 16 years in Washington he complained, "This job guts you. You lose track of what is your real political philosophy. You start voting to maintain your image rather than what you really believe." He felt imprisoned by his past and unable to take the time to explore a different future. In frustration he announced that he would not run for reelection.

Effective time managers are assertive with respect to their environment. They don't just accept the demands imposed on them, but continuously experiment with selectively ignoring certain demands while attempting to renegotiate the terms of others. Most of all, they recognize that they can't be all things to all people, that sometimes they must disappoint some of those who make demands. Key, however, is deciding who and what are given priority.

ON JUGGLING
SEQUENTIALLY
OR SIMULTANEOUSLY
FOCUSING DISCRETIONARY TIME

Reprinted by permission of Unisys Corporation.

There are two kinds of people: sequential people and simultaneous people. Sequential people need to focus on one issue at a time until completion, moving from the first to the second only when the first has been pushed along as far as it can go at the moment. In contrast, simultaneous people are able to juggle multiple balls very closely, sequencing attention to one, then another, then a third, back to the second, to a fourth, back to the first, and so on.

If you are going to be successful as a manager, you had better be a simultaneous person. Most of a manager's time is devoted to responding to various matters and these come simultaneously or very closely sequenced on the average of every three to ten minutes. Unless you have the flexibility to transit rapidly from issue to issue, you are unlikely to be happy or effective as a manager. Better you should be a college professor, a dentist, or independent professional who enjoys greater control of his or her day.

Even the best managers, however, can't always handle problems simultaneously. Sometimes they need to focus and work sequentially on more ambiguous, longer range issues.

Segment and Concentrate: The central message of most advice on time management is segmentation and concentration. Separate response and discretionary time, consolidate discretionary time into longer chunks, and focus discretionary projects in this time. Unfortunately, most managers' discretionary time is so chopped up that it virtually disappears or is unusable. Telephone calls, unexpected visitors, and assorted crises occur so frequently that the manager's day is fractionated. We may underestimate how much discretionary time we potentially possess or find it impossible to start anything substantial for fear of being interrupted.

Reserve Blocks of Time: To utilize discretionary time and progress on a discretionary project requires that time periods be long enough for concentration. The minimum usable time span required by most people to really focus on a complex issue is probably 1½ to 2 hours. Anything less requires too many transitions.

Two-hour chunks are tough to carve out of most weeks. You will really have to fight to schedule them and then to preserve them from interruption. Plan weekly for those periods when you will escape from present demands and focus on longer run discretionary concerns.

Protect Prime Time: "Prime time" is that time when you are most alive and firing on all cylinders. It is the period of the day or week when you are most able to concentrate and be creative. Such time is especially precious.

Humans are cyclic creatures, and most of us are fairly consistent in the periods that are our personal prime times. Some of us are "morning people" and can think most clearly from 6:00 a.m. to 9:00 a.m. Others are "night people" whose brains begin to percolate only with the moon. There is no necessary advantage to being either one or another. What is important, however, is to protect your personal prime time.

Discretionary projects should be scheduled in personal prime time. Thus, you will be handling the most difficult and ambiguous problem solving during your most effective periods. The corollary is to not allow your prime time to be chewed up responding to routine problems. It is better to handle those when you are not at your absolute peak.

Thus, it is probably silly for a morning-type manager to devote mornings to answering mail, especially if the mail deals mainly with routine matters requiring little original thought. It is better to do this late in the afternoon when he or she is running lower on energy and reserve the morning for more difficult matters.

In response time, you will need to be simultaneous. Discretionary time is different, however. Here you should be sequential. That is, you should focus on relatively few discretionary projects during your reserved blocks of time. Don't expect to move ahead on ten different projects during a 90-minute chunk. To attempt to do so will only fractionate your attention as occurs in response time. Transitions from topic to topic will be inefficient and your thinking murky.

A helpful approach for focusing discretionary time is as follows:

1. Each evening draw up your to do list of ten discretionary desirable activities (those activities that you will probably not get to under the press of tomorrow's demands unless you fight for time).
2. Schedule blocks of tomorrow's time for the two highest priority activities on the list.
3. Perform the two activities in the scheduled time. If you complete them and discretionary time is still available, move on to the other activities from last night's list.

A virtue of this approach is modesty. You shouldn't feel defeated if unable to accomplish all the items on a current list. Eighty percent of the total importance in a ten-item list probably is contained in 20 percent of the items. Hence, completing two activities out of a discretionary list of ten will accomplish 80 percent of what was truly important (hopefully).

Exercise Seven

PROGRESSING ON LONGER RANGE, MORE DEFERRABLE GOALS

OBJECTIVES

- to understand the multiple objectives that should characterize all organizations
- to distinguish your most dominant from your more deferrable objectives
- to define what you might do to progress on the longer run, important but easy to defer objectives

CATHY copyright 1981 Cathy Guisewite. Reprinted with permission of UNIVERSAL PRESS SYNDICATE. All rights reserved.

A. EXERCISE—ANALYZING YOUR JOB OBJECTIVES

Locate the objectives of your position along the continuum below of most dominant to most deferrable. Most dominant means that the cues to perform the relevant activities are explicit every day (perhaps minute by minute). You simply must allocate time to them to fulfill your responsibilities. Most deferrable means there are no external cues or they are very subtle and ambiguous. If time is to be devoted to these objectives, you must define and protect it.

MOST DOMINANT OBJECTIVES

■ —

■ —

■ —

■ —

■ —

■ —

■ —

■ —

■ —

■ —

■ —

MOST DEFERRABLE OBJECTIVES

B. EXERCISE—CONTRIBUTING TO MORE DEFERRABLE OBJECTIVES

What activities or projects can I initiate that will contribute to my more deferrable organizational objectives?

1. **Identification (achieving clarity, consensus, and commitment to goals)**

_____
_____
_____
_____
_____

2. **Integration (of employee needs and organizational objectives)**

_____
_____
_____
_____
_____

3. **Influence (distributing power and authority effectively)**

_____
_____
_____
_____
_____

4. **Collaboration (mechanisms for handling conflict)**

_____
_____
_____
_____
_____

5. **Adaptation (monitoring environment and responding appropriately)**

_____
_____
_____
_____
_____

6. **Revitalization (keeping organization flexible and creative)**

_____
_____
_____
_____
_____

C. DISCUSSION—INVESTING TIME IN MORE DEFERRABLE OBJECTIVES

Busy ambitious people desire feedback indicating that they have used their time effectively. But they tend to be impatient. They want results quickly for that is the purpose of their effort and discipline. Unfortunately, excessive concern with rapid progress and feedback can hinder long-range effectiveness. As we've seen, too much attention is directed to the short run without adequate concern for the future.

Effectiveness, however, is more important than efficiency. In time management, means and ends can become confused. The various lists, diaries, logs, and inventories can become ends in themselves if keeping track of time becomes more important than what is done with it. The purpose of the time management strategies is not to save time itself, but to allow time for accomplishing important tasks—and this means tying time to organizational objectives.

Business Objectives: Tomorrow begins with formulation of management's continuing objectives. These are the long-run, ongoing concerns that contain no time limits and no numbers. In some ultimate sense, the central business objective is profit or shareholder value, but no firm will survive unless it pays attention simultaneously to additional objectives.

1. *Profitability/Value:* Market valuation of common stock; or gross profit or net profits, perhaps as a percentage of invested funds.
2. *Market standing:* the proportion of the market enjoyed compared with competitors.
3. *Productivity:* ratio of output of goods or services to input of resources such as labor, material, and money.
4. *State of resources:* protection and maintenance of equipment, buildings, inventory, and financial assets.
5. *Service:* timely and appropriate quality response to customers' and clients' needs.
6. *Innovation:* development and delivery of new products or services.
7. *Social contribution/public responsibility:* improvement of environment and quality of life.

Note that no single set of answers to these objectives is always the best. You could choose to be an innovator or a follower; emphasize service as a competitive tool or discount prices, hide from customers and merely replace products when pressed. You could aim for a full umbrella of products or narrowly specialize. What is important is that the definition of objectives be consistent with your firm's capabilities and the competitive realities of your industry.

Process Objectives: The business objectives just described emphasize results, but we need also to recognize process objectives that apply to business and all other institutions. An organization's success will be limited if time and attention are not allocated to these process objectives.

1. *Identification:* Clarity of purpose cannot be assumed. Attention must be devoted to achieving consensus and commitment to organizational objectives. Top managers should be internal salespeople selling the idea of the organization to its own people.

2. *Integration:* No organization can exist unless its members perceive some overlap between their own personal objectives and those of the firm. This may mean only exchanging their time and muscle for the institution's money, but it generally implies a feeling that at least some needs such as security, affiliation, and esteem are served by contributing to the organization.

3. *Influence:* To facilitate problem solving and goal achievement, all organizations must distribute power and authority. Traditional was power flowing down the hierarchy from the top. But this can no longer be assumed because of greater lower level expectations, increased task complexity, and expanded burdens on the top. Therefore, power distribution should be as planned as other aspects of management.

4. *Collaboration:* No matter how well managed, all organizations of human beings will experience internal conflict. Rather than bemoaning this as a sign of management's failure or personal irrationality, management should see it as another area in which to set objectives. That is, management should institute means of managing conflict (such as grievance procedures, open door policy, corporate ombudsman, due process, and internal organizational development consultants).

5. *Adaptation:* All organizations confront time and environmental changes. Competitors introduce new technology, market tastes change, and new laws are passed that threaten the firm's viability. Accordingly, management needs to define processes for monitoring the external world and internally responding appropriately to threats and opportunities.

6. *Revitalization:* Even if no external threats or opportunities exist, management should strive to exercise the organization's ability to change. This is revitalization. How can we keep the firm light on its feet and able to move if it has to? Admittedly, this is the most subjective objective, but perhaps ultimately the most important.

In the short run, some objectives can be competitive. Simultaneously expanding profits and market share, for example, may be impossible because price cuts may be necessary to attract new customers. And improving productivity and curbing pollution may be mutually exclusive in the short run because pollution control equipment tends to increase costs. When you set goals to be accomplished in a specific time period, you have to deal with this competition among objectives.

Your multiple job objectives can be arrayed along a continuum of "most dominant" to "most deferrable" based on the clarity of the cues precipitating activity on each objective and the time span until measurement for inadequate performance. For example, Exhibit 7-1 illustrates how the 15-person senior management team of Metropolis Electric (name disguised), a large investor owned public power utility, arrayed their objectives.

EXHIBIT 7-1:   Electrical Utility Company Objectives

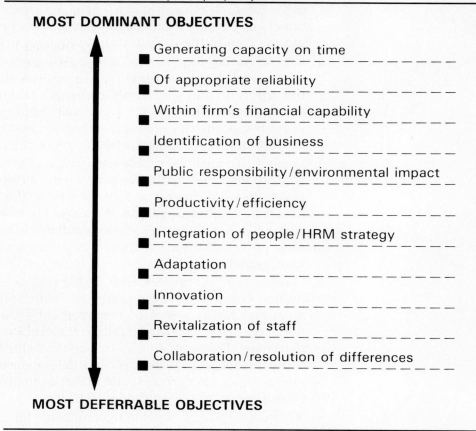

MOST DOMINANT OBJECTIVES

- Generating capacity on time
- Of appropriate reliability
- Within firm's financial capability
- Identification of business
- Public responsibility/environmental impact
- Productivity/efficiency
- Integration of people/HRM strategy
- Adaptation
- Innovation
- Revitalization of staff
- Collaboration/resolution of differences

MOST DEFERRABLE OBJECTIVES

Most dominant are those that demand everyday attention, while deferrable objectives are those that have few explicit cues so that they can be safely ignored for some time. Clearly, the central purpose of this department is to design and construct reliable electrical generation and distribution facilities so that energy consumers in their geographical area will have sufficient energy when needed. And the company must do this within the financial resources available. These are the dominant objectives.

Objectives like adaptation and revitalization were deemed deferrable. The executive team consensus was that these objectives could safely be postponed without immediate adverse impact on performance. Only a voice or two in the group asked whether the company had already delayed too long on these matters, whether in the past too little time had been allocated to these nonspecific objectives so that troubles loomed. Consider one incident. The company lagged in using computers in engineering design. A large mainframe handled payroll, billing, and cost accounting, but the design professionals still used desk calculators and manual drafting. No computer-aided design capability existed. In contrast, designers in advanced electronics firms had computer workstations at their desks. They could call out already designed components from a stored memory, move them around the display screen into a desired configuration, add custom circuitry, push a button, and produce a hard drawing.

To advance the design process, a department manager at the power company decided to hire a design systems expert from a cutting edge electronics firm. He discovered, however, that to hire an experienced person he would have to pay a salary markedly higher than his own. And even if he were willing to pay a subordinate more than he made, the company's personnel policies would not have allowed it. Therefore, the manager hired a junior systems designer who failed because he didn't have sufficient experience, his salary was still higher than most senior engineers, and at the time he had long hair down to his shoulders when most of the middle-aged engineers had crew cuts.

That was a revitalization issue. The firm's policy arteries were so inflexible that they couldn't adapt to labor market realities. Its internal world was out of touch with its environment. The engineering managers' low ranking of revitalization on the most-dominant/most-deferrable continuum is both cause and effect of not carving time out of the present to deal with such long-range matters.

Our company, Metropolis Electric, is not the firm that managed Three Mile Island with its nuclear crisis in 1979, but the executives' assessment of their objectives occurred in the same time period. And the firm's troubles in the ensuing decade were almost predictable from the ignoring of more deferrable objectives. Accidents, operators sleeping on the job, alcohol and drug involvement, and assorted mishaps led in 1988 to the firm's being labeled by the Nuclear Regulatory Commission as a "disgrace to the industry" with subsequent dismissals of the chairman, president, and vice president of Operations.

In my position as university vice president for development and university relations, three more deferrable, long-range objectives were particularly important: identification, revitalization, and integration.

- *Identification—Focusing on the central and shared rather than the separate.* Some large, complex, multi-schooled universities suffer from affluence in the professional and health school parts, but poverty in the core arts and sciences programs as well as in shared academic resources such as libraries. Corporate support is increasingly being restricted to specific programs deemed most important to the donor's interests. And alumni may identify more with the part of the university that they attended or with the program closest to their vocation. As a result, support for the core resources that bind such a university together can lag.

  To counter this trend, I felt it necessary repeatedly (*ad nauseum* to many I'm sure) to emphasize that the whole is more important than any single part; that any undergraduate alumnus/alumna is first a graduate of the university and not primarily of the particular school; and that we can't assume that an alumnus/alumna will only be interested in his or her undergraduate school. We should communicate the mission of the whole institution to all potentially interested parties prior to their identifying a particular part as a special interest. And even if a potential donor narrows his or her perspective, that person should be gently and persistently reminded of the whole through words and images that emphasize the connectedness of the institution.

In terms of the activity analysis in Exercise Two, this is a "time not a factor" activity of which I should always be aware in order to repeat the message and take advantage of unplanned opportunities to present core possibilities.

- *Revitalization—Generating development investment funds.* My university's fund raising and public relations opportunities sharply exceeded my department's budgetary resources. Using our resources to maximum efficiency and strengthening our case for increased allocation from the president was critical. Nonetheless, I came to feel that running our operation solely on funds appropriated by the president would never supply enough resources. Perceived competition for limited dollars among all administrative departments; academic distrust of more funds for central administration; and a policy forbidding soliciting gifts directly for development use would always put us in an excessively restricted posture.

  A continuing objective, then, became broadening the source of development's resources. What are the theoretical alternatives? How did other schools do it? What are the political advantages and disadvantages of different approaches? So here we have another "time not a factor" objective, although deadlines can be set for specific steps to push along the objective (e.g., canvas fellow vice presidents at other schools; call the Council for Advancement and Support of Education in Washington, DC to see if they have any information; and draft a think-piece for the president to consider).

- *Integration—Provide performance-based rewards.* As fund raising has become more competitive and sophisticated, more ambitious, energetic, and creative people become essential. The "good old alum," the "semi-retired executive," and the "failed professor" simply are no longer sufficient unless they have the necessary personal qualities. Unfortunately, educational institutions sometimes have neither the resources nor the will to pay the salaries necessary to attract and hold such people. University salary administrators understandably have difficulty responding to market conditions with 33-year-old fund raisers making more money than 50-year-old professors. Even more profoundly, schools are loath to allow bonuses that reflect annual performance. They fear complaints of inequity that campus knowledge of such awards might produce.

  This anxiety is understandable and I certainly have not discovered a solution to the dilemma. Nonetheless, I saw as a continuing long-run objective the implementation of bonuses to exceptional fund raisers. About all I accomplished, however, was simply raising the issue. But even that wouldn't occur unless time was carved out of the short run to research and argue for the proposal.

In summary, effective strategic time managers are always aware of their more deferrable but important longer range objectives for which they need to find short-run investment time.

ON THE GOD COMPLEX
MAINTAINING MANAGERIAL
RESPONSIVENESS

From the Wall Street Journal, reprinted by permission of Cartoon Features Syndicate

Consider the mental patient who suffers from what psychiatry calls "the God complex." Only *his* time is valuable in comparison with others, *his* time is correct, *he* alone is justified in being unpunctual, and his prediction of future events will alone be fulfilled. Similar distortion is a danger for most hard-charging executives. In striving to improve their management of time, they must avoid becoming too self-centered in assuming that allocation of their time is *the* critical variable in the organization.

A company president complains that 70 percent of his time is spent just listening and half that time is "wasted on things you'd avoid if you had any way of appraising them in advance." But, to conclude that time is wasted *just because it is used in an unplanned way* is a distortion of values, a misguided over-concern for time at the expense of the job. Back of this distortion seems to be an unspoken assumption that unless a manager controls his or her own behavior and does only what he or she intends to do, he or she is wasting time. Even in a profit-seeking business, this is an exaggeration bordering on absurdity.

Being Available: High executives initiate many inquiries and conversations. In spite of the importance of initiating communications, however, they depend even more on others bringing information to them. They must be open and receptive to communications from subordinates and associates. That this is an effective style is suggested by our finding that *high-rated executives spend more time than lower-rated executives advising and discussing with people who come to them*. Those considered more effective devote some 16 hours per week talking in response to others' initiation. The less effective executives spend only 9 hours per week responding.

In contrast, the lower-rated executives initiate over 11 hours per week of conversation, while the more effective initiate only about 6 hours per week. Apparently, effective executives develop their various relationships so that others feel free to come to them.

Shortly after the death of Winston Churchill, his former Foreign Minister Anthony Eden discussed what he considered Churchill's outstanding leadership characteristic. He said that the indefatigable former Prime Minister always seemed to be available and ready to listen. He never cut off a suggestion with a curt dismissal, but encouraged elaboration. To be sure, the great man was often abusive to subordinates who made mistakes in policy implementation. And he could be dictatorial in ordering the conduct of his own policy. Nonetheless, he was invariably receptive to new ideas. It was not a threatening experience to broach a new matter to Churchill. The next day he might assert that the proposal was unacceptable, but the initial presentation was respected. Consequently, he was approached—and some of the unsolicited ideas were good. It appears that similar behavior characterizes effective business executives.

Being Responsive: Mentally separating response time from your own discretionary time assists in maintaining responsiveness to others. Managers must accept that certain periods will be primarily response time. They may work on discretionary matters if no one contacts them, but should not expect to accomplish very much. If they do, it is an unexpected bonus. This orientation toward response will help to overcome the natural irritation of having outside events interfere with self-determined plans. Thus, self-discipline is essential to create a climate of openness and responsiveness.

Managers should strive to project an unrushed image; fight to avoid seeming preoccupied with their own concerns; and give subordinates their undivided attention. No one expects perfect attention every time, but sometimes it is imperative. A subordinate's respect for himself and for his superior will be undermined without it. Research also suggests that effective *executives conduct more of their numerous discussions in intimate two-person talks than in group meetings or via correspondence*. They seem to throw out invitations for individuals to come see them personally rather than waiting for the next scheduled meeting. Obviously, this is an untidy way to operate. It consumes much precious time. Yet, executives undoubtedly derive benefits from a two-person style: it facilitates the frank expression of opinions and ideas that they so desire, with less danger of antagonizing others who might be present in a group meeting.

Availability to subordinates and associates recognizes that managers must be responsive or they will lose touch with their organizations. They cannot possibly initiate enough interactions to maintain control. Being there on the scene and available is a necessity because timing is so important. If the executive is not available when needed to supply information or support, subordinates just may lose interest.

Exercise Eight

INVESTING
IN INTERPERSONAL
RELATIONSHIPS

OBJECTIVES

- to determine the people with whom you communicate
- to avoid having routine tasks and unpredictable emergencies totally dictate who they are
- to analyze in which relationships you should invest time and how frequently

CATHY copyright 1991 Cathy Guisewite. Reprinted with permission of UNIVERSAL PRESS SYNDICATE. All rights reserved.

A. EXERCISE—ANALYZING YOUR COMMUNICATIONS

Write the names of people with whom you communicate at work across the four columns below.

People I should talk with every day	People I should talk with or write to frequently	People to talk with or write to regularly	People to communicate with only when necessary

B. DISCUSSION—INVESTING IN RELATIONSHIPS

No one should allow the week's routines or the day's emergencies to determine totally the people with whom they communicate. Effective strategic time managers systematically invest time in building and maintaining long-term relationships. These are not the daily telephone calls or letters that would be on today's to do list. Rather, these are investment communications. Others may resent us for always expecting them to respond when we have invested little in building a relationship or in offering them opportunities to draw on our advice or service. Perhaps even more importantly, we are not likely to discover those people who share our values or vision of the institution—in short, those people who might be allies in some unknown future debate.

EXHIBIT 8-1: Communications Analysis for Vice President for Development and University Relations

People I should talk to every day

- *my executive secretary*
- *director of development*
- *department budget director*
- *my assistant to the vice president*
- *director of development systems*

People to talk to (or write to) at least weekly

- *university president*
- *president's executive assistant*
- *executive director of university budget*
- *director alumni relations*
- *director major gifts*
- *director annual giving*
- *editor campus administration newspaper*
- *president's secretary*
- *university provost*
- *director university relations*
- *director news bureau*
- *associate director major gifts*
- *university director federal relations*

People to talk to (or write to) at least monthly

- *university senior vice president business*
- *university director wage and salary*
- *university vice president finance*
- *university treasurer*
- *director university planning*
- *deans of major schools*
- *major schools development directors*
- *vice provost university life*
- *trustee chair of development committee*
- *chair of trustees*
- *editor faculty newspaper*
- *university vice president human resources*
- *university vice president operational services*
- *university vice president medical affairs*
- *director publications*
- *dean of admissions*
- *director athletics*
- *vice provost for research*
- *university counsel*
- *trustee chair of relations committee*
- *editor alumni magazine*
- *chair faculty senate*

People to talk to (or write to) at least once an academic year

- *50 most important donors*
- *all trustees*
- *athletic advisory council*
- *attendees of all cultivation events*
- *chair student government*
- *chairs of regional development committees*
- *all dept. profess. staff*
- *vps of league schools*
- *editor student newspaper*

Young Senator Lyndon B. Johnson would leave his office several times a day to go to the lavatory. Rather than using his own private facility adjacent to his office, he would walk around the Senate office building. These rambles were not random. They precipitated meeting people "accidentally on purpose." Thus, he tried to frequently chat with senior members of the then Senate establishment like Richard Russell and Walter George of Georgia from whom he could gain informal advice on difficult situations—as well as paying the elder senator a compliment while drawing attention to himself. Upon returning to his desk, he would cross off their names on his daily to do lists.

A cynic might refer to this as "office politiking," "apple polishing," "brown nosing," or terms more odious, but a more charitable perspective is to see it as investing short-run time in building long-term relationships (which in Johnson's case saw him elected the youngest Senate majority leader in history). In business, less successful young professionals and managers passively allow their current tasks to determine what they learn and with whom they communicate. In contrast, the more effective actively explore the organization by developing and maintaining relationships with a wider variety of people—in short, going out of the way and spending precious short-run time in the interest of the long run.

Note that communications analysis refers to both "talking" and "writing." Small handwritten notes of thanks and congratulations are powerful techniques for building and maintaining relationships. President George Bush invests significant time in writing such notes as an investment in his political alliances on which he can draw during times of extraordinary challenge. The very time inefficiency in handwriting the notes is what gives them their power.

Exhibit 8-1 illustrates my own application of this analysis (substituting position titles for names). For me, "frequently" means weekly, "regularly" means monthly, and "infrequently," a vaguer something in this semester or academic year. In the positions listed, I've distinguished between subordinates, other university staff, and outsiders.

Note how important I felt it was to maintain relationships with certain administrators who in the normal course of events I would see only infrequently. For example, I tried to chat with the president's executive director of the budget at least once a week. In terms of task, we were intensely involved with each other only about a month during the annual budget process. But that process was likely to be more effective if we shared our concerns about the university away from the pressures of pie dividing. Similarly, I tried to "bump into" the deans of the most critical schools in order to provide opportunity to defuse issues that could fester if they had to await scheduling a formal meeting.

Many of the positions listed are of course people within my own department whom I would undoubtedly see whether or not I made such a specific analysis. Nonetheless, thinking about it did encourage me to set up standing meetings to ensure that I initiated some long-range investment communications every day (even if on particularly busy days they consisted only of a handwritten note to a manager with whom I had strained relations, perhaps with a relevant clipping or cartoon from the morning newspaper). The key is exercising the communications lines, especially with the people you would rather avoid.

ON HORIZONTAL
AND VERTICAL PEOPLE
TACTICS FOR AVOIDING A STACKED DESK

Drawing by Barsotti; © The New Yorker Magazine, Inc. Reprinted by permission.

Are you a horizontal or vertical person? Horizontal people like to be surrounded at work by flat areas—large desk, table, shelves. On this horizontal area are stacked various piles of folders, papers, memos, and the like. Each pile represents a major job responsibility or discretionary project. As a horizontal person gazes over these various piles, he or she can form a mental picture of what is to be done. The piles are visual reminders.

Unfortunately, these piles on a stacked desk can also waste time by interfering with concentration and communication. Each stack can be seen as a little radio transmitter sending out messages that trigger the receiver in your brain. And they can be sending simultaneously! As you look up from the work immediately before you on your desk, your attention can be distracted by the waves from each pile. And each pile represents dreams, problems, and anxieties that nag at you for a shorter or longer time as you try to return to your immediate work. These mini-transitions undermine your efficiency and waste time.

And it is even worse when someone is trying to talk to you across the piles. Your attention may wander as your eyes alight on a pile. Or anxiety about your pending volume of work can inadvertently cause you to communicate your harriedness to your visitor, shuffling papers, playing with a pencil, or repeatedly glancing at your watch.

Such inattention and harriedness may discourage people from initiating talks. Worse, you may actually be glad to be left alone to concentrate on your piles or contemplate your pictures. But the cost can be heavy because you may be cut off from essential information. You will learn only what you ask about specifically. Little that is spontaneous will come your way if your visitors feel they are only interrupting.

It is better to be a vertical person. Such a person keeps folders in a file cabinet until needed. The only material on his or her desk is that being worked on at the moment. If you are unable to limit yourself to such files and you simply must have horizontal space, it is better to have it behind your desk so you and your visitors don't have to peer through it or over it. It would be better yet if the piles can be hidden by a curtain when people are meeting in your office.

A third technique exists, a combined horizontal and vertical approach. This consists of keeping material in hanging folders on wire frames placed on shelves. Maintaining the discipline to refile as work proceeds appears to be much easier when files are so open rather than closed away in file drawers out of sight and mind. The hanging folders present a much neater appearance and they can be hidden by sliding or folding doors.

This is not a trivial detail. Concentration will be stronger and communication more effective if you and your office convey an atmosphere of serenity and non-time-harriedness.

Exercise Nine

PRACTICING
YOUR ABILITY
TO CHANGE

OBJECTIVES

- to fight the tendency with time and success to become inflexible and obsolescent
- to pinpoint some job tasks with which you can experiment with change
- to invest time in personal development activities that exercise your ability to perceive closely and uniquely

CATHY copyright 1990 Cathy Guisewite. Reprinted with permission of UNIVERSAL PRESS SYNDICATE. All rights reserved.

A. EXERCISE—DEFINING YOUR PERSONAL REVITALIZATION ACTIVITIES

List two or three activities under each of the following three quarterly or semi-annual objectives.

---

1. Job Innovation. On what activities can you experiment with changing how you do them? What might you try?

---

2. Personal Growth. What activities might you invest in that would expand your knowledge or observational skill?

---

3. Personal Mastery. What intimate personal behavior might you change in the interest of better physical or psychological health?

B. DISCUSSION—STRATEGIES FOR STAYING VITAL

Habit and preoccupation are the ultimate threats of success. As we master our jobs and grow older, we tend to behave without thinking, sort of sleepwalking through our lives, allowing our perceptive skills to atrophy. Fiftyish men particularly demonstrate a propensity to insulate themselves—to draw back from the competitive fray, to lose touch with customers and markets. One study of 2,000 executives concluded that the single most important attribute of those who handled success well (and were able to maintain it) was their ability to embrace change. To stay so vital requires maintaining the ability to perceive uniquely, to see *differences*.

Experience can be a great source of learning of course. It can certainly save a lot of time as we fit current problems into the learned categories from the past. Unfortunately, it can also waste time and cause disaster if we categorize prematurely and erroneously.

You have heard of people who have worked for 20 years, but don't have 20 years' experience. They merely repeated the first year 20 times. Such people may treat a new problem as if it were like past problems, but in fact it is new and unique. Keeping alive this ability to perceive deeply requires frequent exercise. This means building into our daily life regular repetition of the process of letting go of the known and confronting the unknown—change for the hell of it. This doesn't require quitting your job, divorcing your spouse, and moving to Hawaii. Rather, it means frequent small encounters with threatening changes.

Job Innovation.   Every three to six months you might focus on one major aspect of your job and put it on trial for its life. Could it be eliminated? Could it simply be ignored until someone complains? Or could you experiment with changing it? As Exhibit 9-1 illustrates, in applying this tactic to my own work, the task that jumped out at me was grading. After 15 years as a teacher, I was experiencing increasing difficulty in evaluating student papers. I found myself giving no F's or D's and almost no C's. Everyone was getting a B or an A. Had I become too lax? Had I been corrupted by the grading inflation that affected schools everywhere? Did I court student popularity so avidly that I wanted everyone to be happy? Or was I such an outstanding teacher that all my students were able to master the material?

I would have liked to answer the last question in the affirmative, but I needed to probe deeper. What could I change? Perhaps I could give no tests or require no papers (sure to be popular with students, but a cop-out of a teacher's responsibility). Or perhaps I could delegate all grading to a graduate student assistant who could deal with unhappy students (tempting, but likewise irresponsible in my opinion). Or, perhaps I could have changed my testing format. Because I believed that life is an open book rather than a closed book examination, I gave only take-home cases and essay questions that required students to write fairly lengthy reports (which are of course easier to read than scribbled in-class quizzes). But grading such reports is quite subjective. It was often difficult to defend my judgment when an ambitious student complained. Perhaps I could have changed my method. Other professors use a more objective true–false or multiple choice format. Such tests are easier to grade and seem to provide more defensible numbers as grades.

EXHIBIT 9-1:   Sample of Quarterly Personal Revitalization Activities

Job Innovation
- *method of evaluating student performance*
- *resume teaching undergraduates*
- *learn to write on the computer*

Personal Growth
- *take waterpainting lessons*
- *enroll in an Italian language course*
- *learn to ski*

Personal Mastery
- *eliminate ice cream and reduce to one cola per day*
- *lift weights and work out four days per week*

This specific example of my personal grading problem is obviously not important to most readers (and will not elicit your sympathy, I'm sure), but the point is that we all have central aspects of our jobs on which we experience difficulty. I once asked a group of managers at one of the world's best managed firms what activity they found most difficult—so much so that it was the number one thing on which they procrastinated. Their most common reply was giving a negative performance evaluation, particularly to a subordinate older in age than the evaluating manager.

They want to avoid an unpleasant confrontation, or they don't believe the older person would change anyway, or they are not confident of their performance criteria. What they might do is focus on one or two older, unsatisfactory subordinates for a few months, experimenting with changing the mode of performance feedback. Perhaps they could write a memo to themselves *every* time they observe the subordinate in action. Then they could schedule time *every* week to discuss these observations while they are fresh rather than letting unrecorded impressions pile up until a fruitless annual interview ritual. The new approach may or may not work, but the very action of confronting a difficult new behavior will help preserve your vitality.

Personal Growth: Most creative ideas don't spring fully defined from the creator's mind like Botticelli's Venus springing from the sea. Rather, most creativity is borrowing something from one context and applying it to another. So more creative people tend to have wider and more random interests outside their specialization. Quarterly or semi-annual personal growth objectives are intended to encourage you to focus on a new field or activity—learning how to play the piano at age 35; studying Spanish at age 40; starting to paint at 50. All can be vehicles for keeping alive your ability to perceive uniquely.

I had been painting pictures with oil paints for many years when I decided to try watercolors. What to the uninitiated appears as a trivial shift turned out to require very different observational skills. Oil painting for me is a spontaneous medium in which errors are easy to correct by simply painting over the offending portion. The smell and feel of the semi-solid paint is very *physical*. Waterpainting turned out to be entirely different. It is so planned and intellectual. What is key is where on the paper you *don't* paint—the whites are much of the finished picture. And errors can not be covered up; the paint is too transparent. Consequently, the entire painting must be planned in advance in great detail so the scene being painted must be studied much more deeply than when oil painting. It is precisely this intense study that is the purpose of periodic personal growth objectives that involve modest but repeated confrontations with the unknown. In these encounters it is less important that you actually master the new than that you give it a good effort.

Personal Mastery: The final periodic target is what improvement you might make in your diet, physical activity, or recreation. What can you do at the most personal level to improve your well-being? As the founder of my university, Benjamin Franklin, told us long ago, mastering your own eating, exercise and play habits can provide a tonic to your total life situation. Being in control of yourself in mid-life will spill over onto the job and improve your task mastery and flexibility.

My own first application of this maintenance objective led to the virtual elimination of soft drinks from my diet. Long a cola freak (since I didn't drink coffee, I had to find something containing caffeine to keep me awake in college and the navy), I consumed more than six cans a day. Since I hated the taste of sugar substitutes, that is a lot of refined sugar. The reduced sugar intake was desirable and the 20-pound weight loss rewarding, but even more beneficial was the verification that I could do it.

The major purpose of all these tactics is to help maturing managers to perceive situations as unique, to retain their ability to see how the present is different from the past, and how the future will be different still. As you grow older, you need to retain a tolerance for ambiguity, which will help you avoid the ultimate time wastage of mindlessly repeating yourself.

ON MANAGERIAL SLEEPWALKING
TACTICS FOR AVOIDING
BEING TYRANNIZED
BY YOUR PAST

Drawing by Levin; © 1978 The New Yorker Magazine, Inc.

The past is seductive, but often tyrannizing. Because certain behavior has worked, we continue it even when the world has changed and the past ways no longer fit.

Persistence of Inappropriate Behavior: Consider the following tale about the British Army. After France fell to the invading German Army in 1940, England felt invasion was imminent. Guns were in short supply and the British pressed into service some venerable formerly horse-drawn artillery pieces left over from the turn of the century Boer War. Hitched to light trucks, the guns would be hauled up and down the channel coast, and various test firings were held at night. The English hoped to mislead Nazi intelligence into concluding that they had more artillery than actually was the case.

Unfortunately, the gun was extremely slow firing. Therefore, a time study expert was brought in to determine how the firing rate could be improved. The engineer observed a five-man crew in action and took some slow-motion pictures. Studying the actions of the young soldiers, he noticed something odd: a moment before firing, two members ceased all movement and came to attention for a three-second interval extending through the firing of the weapon. He consulted an elderly colonel of artillery who was also puzzled but finally exclaimed, "I have it! They are holding the horses." The horses, of course, had long since gone the way of the Boer War and the youthful soldiers had not even been born when horses pulled the guns. But the old procedures were still being followed without thought—even though they were incongruous to the present.

Tactics for Overcoming the Past: You should fight the tendency to sleepwalk through your job unaware of what you are doing. Some specific tactics can help in this battle.

1. Tear up job descriptions. Every couple of years you might shred your own and subordinates' job descriptions. Propose new ones. Don't revise the old; write anew. Each rewrite will demand a fresh look at duties and a more relevant statement of behavior.

2. Mix up your files. Each few years, remove the category labels from your files, shuffle the folders, and refile. Such intentional chaos will demand that you examine each file to determine if it really should be maintained.

3. Keep a daily diary for a month. Doing so will be a pain, but it won't be permanent. You need data on where your time actually goes and what cues you are responding to. At the end of the month subject every entry to the questions: Did I have to perform that activity? Could the cue be ignored the next time? In short, eliminate what doesn't clearly justify itself. Repeat the exercise every two years.

4. Write memos to yourself for a year. After major job events, write yourself a short memo describing what went right or wrong and why. These are not self-protection notes to be trotted out when under interrogation. They are for your own eyes only to be used to learn from your past in a systematic way. On vacation while stretched out on the sand, you could peruse the year's accumulation of memos. Look for patterns of success or failure. What mistakes do you tend to repeat? Do you forget to keep your boss informed? Do you repeatedly jump to conclusions too quickly? The trick is to detect how you repeat the same mistakes over and over. As Justice Oliver Wendell Holmes once exclaimed, "Three generations of idiots are enough!"

5. Change for the sake of change. Every three to six months, focus on one major job responsibility. Leave most of your job as is, but experiment with some change in one area even if present behavior seems unsatisfactory. For example, you could focus on your performance feedback to subordinates. Experiment with keeping a critical incident diary. Or consider different forms and interviews.

6. Repeatedly confront the unknown. Challenge and variety off the job can help you to maintain on-the-job alertness. Such confrontation is not random, however. It should be disciplined practice of an activity that demands close attention. Studying Italian in your thirties, learning to paint with water colors in your forties, practicing the piano in your fifties. All can help you preserve the ability to perceive uniquely, to avoid premature categorization, to see differences in middle age where others see sameness.

7. Remain alive to chance. Creative people tend to have more varied sources of information than many of us. They read more widely and randomly in fields outside their vocations. They expose themselves to more varied stimuli which are helpful in solving problems. Most creativity doesn't spring full blown from the creator's mind, but reflects borrowing from one setting to another.

8. Master yourself on small matters. A French philosopher-statesman once asked, "How shall I be able to rule over others if I have not full power and command of myself?" Seers as diverse as Saint Francis and Ben Franklin have argued that little acts of discipline can influence all of life with a sense of confidence. And this holds also for time management. Changing your route to work, walking up stairs rather than riding the elevator, peddling a bike rather than some driving, giving up most of your daily coffee or cola. Such changes in exercise and diet can invigorate your ability to overcome habit and escape from the past.

Some of these tactics can be frightening, of course. A great teacher periodically throws out his class notes to force himself to rewrite them. Otherwise, he might fall into the trap of repeating them unto irrelevance. But what an act of courage! As a professor, it gives me butterflies since much of my life is in my files. Nonetheless, that courageous teacher is correct.

Exercise Ten

PUSHING AHEAD SIMULTANEOUSLY ON SHORTER AND LONGER TERM OBJECTIVES

OBJECTIVES

- to remind you of the need to carve time out of the present to invest in longer term objectives
- to provide a daily time management form that will assist you in balancing your varied activities

Reprinted by permission: Tribune Media Services

A. EXERCISE—USING A DAILY PLANNING FORM

Utilize the following form for a week.

Monday

Communications	Activities
1. Meetings and Isolation Time	**2. Most Dominant** **(must be done today)**
8:00	
9:00	
10:00	
11:00	
12:00	
1:00	
2:00	
3:00	
4:00	
5:00	
6:00	
4. Interpersonal Investment **Other people to see,** **telephone, or write to**	**3. Activities to Promote** **More Deferrable Objectives**

5. Personal Revitalization Activities

Tuesday

Communications	Activities
1. Meetings and Isolation Time	**2. Most Dominant** (must be done today)
8:00	
9:00	
10:00	
11:00	
12:00	
1:00	
2:00	
3:00	
4:00	
5:00	
6:00	
4. Interpersonal Investment Other people to see, telephone, or write to	**3. Activities to Promote** More Deferrable Objectives

5. Personal Revitalization Activities

Wednesday

Communications	Activities
1. Meetings and Isolation Time	**2. Most Dominant** (must be done today)
8:00	
9:00	
10:00	
11:00	
12:00	
1:00	
2:00	
3:00	
4:00	
5:00	
6:00	
4. Interpersonal Investment Other people to see, telephone, or write to	**3. Activities to Promote** More Deferrable Objectives

5. Personal Revitalization Activities

Thursday

Communications	Activities
1. Meetings and Isolation Time	**2. Most Dominant** **(must be done today)**
8:00	
9:00	
10:00	
11:00	
12:00	
1:00	
2:00	
3:00	
4:00	
5:00	
6:00	
4. Interpersonal Investment **Other people to see,** **telephone, or write to**	**3. Activities to Promote** **More Deferrable Objectives**

5. Personal Revitalization Activities

Friday

Communications	Activities
1. Meetings and Isolation Time	**2. Most Dominant** (must be done today)
8:00	
9:00	
10:00	
11:00	
12:00	
1:00	
2:00	
3:00	
4:00	
5:00	
6:00	
4. Interpersonal Investment Other people to see, telephone, or write to	**3. Activities to Promote** More Deferrable Objectives

5. Personal Revitalization Activities

B. DISCUSSION—INCORPORATING THE LONG RUN INTO DAILY SCHEDULES

Effective time managers are adept at near-simultaneity: that is, pushing ahead on short-run and long-run issues on a daily and weekly basis. They are not perfect, of course, and sometimes daily routine and weekly emergencies totally dominate, but generally, the key is maintaining progress on longer range, more deferrable matters while still handling the short run.

Exercise Ten suggests a daily time management form designed to remind you of the multiple fronts on which you as a manager should be progressing simultaneously. Section 1 in the upper left is for entering scheduled meetings whether long-term standing meetings or those of more exceptional variety. Standing meetings are commitments in advance to protect time for meeting with a specific individual or group, perhaps even a year in advance. I strongly advocate standing meetings because they have several advantages:

1. Standing meetings symbolically communicate the importance you place on meeting with the people involved. For example, I would not accept my university president's invitation for me to become vice president of development and university relations until he committed to a two-hour meeting with me every other week for a full year in advance. I needed this as verification of the priority he would place on public relations and fund raising.

2. Standing meetings also can reduce interruptions by encouraging you and others to save your questions and comments—perhaps by simply depositing reminder notes into a folder marked with the other person's name. When the time for the standing meeting arrives, you virtually have an agenda in the notes collected in that person's folder. This doesn't mean, of course, that one can't call the other when necessary, but it can reduce interruptions.

3. Finally, standing meetings serve as self-discipline to communicate with certain people that you might rather avoid because you don't like them or you find the topics unpleasant. Standing meetings can be a pain because they clog your calendar and reduce personal flexibility. Nonetheless, in my view their advantages outweigh their disadvantages.

This upper left section can also be used to block out those time periods when you want insulation and isolation for chunks of time to focus on more ambiguous and deferrable tasks.

The upper right section 2, Most Dominant Activities, is where you can write the regular daily to do list for all those things that must be done today.

Section 3 for More Deferrable activities is smaller, of course, because the most dominant by definition will consume most of most days. Nonetheless, this section is very important for it represents what you can do today to push ahead on long-range, more-deferrable (but very important) objectives like innovation, revitalization, and collaboration discussed in Exercise Seven.

Section 4 is to remind you of the need to invest time in building and maintaining long-term relationships discussed in Exercise Eight.

Finally, the last section on the Daily Time Plan, section 5, is for personal revitalization activities that will probably receive too little attention anyway, but get none unless, as suggested in Exercise Nine, you give them dignity equal to your job's demands. When I accepted my position as university vice president, I immediately acquired a gym locker which I promised myself I would use three times a week in order to maintain my stamina and recharge my competitive juices. Unfortunately, in almost five years, I never used it once! May you be more successful.

Using such a daily form seems like a lot of work and time, but it is really not much more than most everyone's daily to do lists and calendars consume. It just gets everything in one place. And this can be invaluable for providing data to periodically review in order to question what you've done as well as to guide decisions on what you *shouldn't* do in the future. The chief executive of Pacific Telesis has developed the custom of reviewing on Sunday evenings everything he did during the previous week. Before laying aside the past week's agenda and looking over the coming week's, he asks himself: "Why did I do all these things?" The resulting answers often lead to changes in how he handles future time. As he says, "There is no point in trying to manage your time unless you're willing to change the way you spend it."

It is precisely such willingness to change that is at the heart of being an effective strategic time manager and thus breaking the time barrier.

ON CONFRONTING
TIME ANXIETY
GUIDELINES FOR TIME HAUNTED PEOPLE

Reprinted by special permission of Playboy Magazine: © 1980 by Playboy.

Some time anxiety is not unhealthy. Indeed, it is very helpful in generating the sense of urgency so essential to accomplishing anything important. Being an effective manager requires some degree of time hauntedness.

Still, the anxiety can be excessive. The stress can incur steep psychosomatic costs. Here are some simple exercises designed to help you confront time in daily life. Not esoteric Zen-like rituals, these everyday behaviors can assist you to accept the reality of passing time with reduced anxiety. Basic achievement drive remains unhampered.

1. When waiting for your airplane to begin loading, don't rush to the gate immediately after the announcement to board. Rather, sit and wait until most other passengers have gone aboard. Your seat is reserved; there is no point in waiting in line and you can control it.

2. Similarly, when deplaning, don't bounce out of your seat even before the jet has pulled up to the gate. Sit and enjoy the rather silly spectacle of fellow passengers jostling each other in order to save three minutes (and not even that if you have checked luggage to fetch).

3. Extend this practice to other settings. Don't leave the ball game in the eighth inning or the concert in the middle of the last selection in order to "beat the crowd." You can be the last one out of the theatre. You will lose very little actual time and it will feel luxurious.

4. As you approach a bridge toll station, don't frantically and dangerously shift lanes seeking the shortest line. Rather, accept the line most convenient, even if it is the longest. While crawling to the gate, observe the people in the other cars around you. Their antics can be very entertaining.

5. Minimize running to catch your bus or subway even if walking might increase your chance of missing it. If you do miss it, you could have an unexpected tidbit of time, a gift that might be used. At any rate, you will feel more civilized.

6. Don't exceed the highway speed limit. Driving at 55 miles per hour is the law of course, but it also greatly facilitates noticing what you are driving by. And while commuting, you might occasionally drive a different, perhaps longer and less trafficked route. It will be a small adventure that relaxes the tension of elapsed travel time.

7. Walking or bicycling can have the same beneficial effect (in addition to health advantages). Awareness of the slower transportation mode can encourage you to plan ahead for adequate time to reach your destination. Allowing more time tends to reduce the feeling of time pressure.

8. If you are a boat person, try sailing instead of power cruising. Sailing puts you in touch with natural forces that elicit modesty about human power. And sailing forces you to confront time, to accept that certain activities just can't be hurried.

9. Sometimes perform household chores in an old-fashioned manual way. Hand washing the dishes can be a satisfying experience once in a while (you really have to pay attention or you break them!).

10. Don't wear your watch on weekends. Not having your watch on your wrist will make it impossible to continually consult it as time-anxious people are inclined to do.

The point of these trivial-appearing suggestions is training yourself to reject slavery to time's tyranny in life's small aspects. You don't have to always hurry up and wait. Fighting time here is a habit that can be broken. Plenty of big time pressures exist about which you can do little. Controlling the small things, however, can permeate your whole life, making the big problems seem more manageable.

No magical techniques exist for creating minutes out of nothing or eliminating all waste from one's personal hours. Self-management for executives, managers, and professionals is rooted in the most fundamental issues of personal goals and organizational objectives. Like dieting and exercising, it seems, effective self-management demands facing tough decisions with a sense of what you *really* want to accomplish.

Improving executive self-management begins with an examination of time wasters. What are the persistent factors that cause people to drift? Three broad categories stand out: the dominance of the present, the tyranny of the past, and the ambiguity of the future.

Short-run time wastage stems from unpredictable events to which an overburdened manager must respond—visitors, telephone calls, equipment breakdowns, personnel emergencies, meetings that start late and drag on interminably, and so on. We all recognize our personal burglars there. These events in themselves, however, are not the villains. After all, responding to such matters is part of being a person in authority. The problem is that they chew up time into tiny bits, throwing managers into a response mode from which initiation is difficult. Present responsiveness dominates behavior because discretionary time is broken into such small chunks that one cannot concentrate on discretionary, future-oriented matters. An executive can be trapped in the present, growing increasingly out of touch with his or her own goals and ignorant of external developments—until midlife crisis emerges or an overwhelming outside threat looms.

Fighting for short-run survival when facing unpredictable and overwhelming events can be seductively eased by accepting the tyranny of the past. By blindly following past policies, procedures, and practices, you can become more "time efficient" because you have standing "answers" to recurring problems. Of course, this is not all bad; a manager would be foolish to ignore history's lessons by treating every issue as unique, thereby repeatedly reinventing the wheel. The problem is that these past categories may no longer be relevant to the present issues. We doggedly fit present circles into past squares, sleepwalking through our jobs.

The dominance of the present and the tyranny of the past are fearsome time wasters, but they pale in significance before the ambiguity of the future. Just as economists tell us that hard money drives out soft, programmed tasks tend to force out the unprogrammed. Most of us would rather work long and diligently (and perhaps even "efficiently") on definite tasks that we understand rather than confront the ambiguity of conceptualizing different tasks and different objectives. Consequently, we don't fight for the discretionary time to examine more fundamental factors that waste huge gobs of calendar time.

The cliché of our times is that the only unchanging fact is change itself. We Americans are remarkably willing to change, but not blindly and not without stress. Much time is lost in organizations because change agent-managers peruse an illusion of painless change: change in which others will change their behavior while the change agent does not, change where the executive doesn't have to be the bad guy upsetting people. The reality is that effective and lasting change requires the executive to present an appropriate model in his or her personal behavior, especially in ability to absorb the antagonism of others.

Tactics and strategies for self-management must fit the three main causes of time wastage. To combat the dominance of the present, various techniques exist such as grouping, insulation, isolation, segmentation, concentration, single handling, time inventories, and quiet hours. Escape from the tyranny of the past is sought through strategies of elimination, justification, not prematurely categorizing, facilitating chance events, and confronting new challenges—in fact, some change just for the sake of change. Confronting the future's ambiguities can be encouraged through delegation and developing a repertoire of tactics for handling role stress such as partial withdrawal, selective ignorance, pragmatic expedience, and courageous confrontation.

In total, breaking your time barrier is built on a philosophy of periodically giving up the known and confronting the unknown because it is in such confrontation that humans retain flexibility and courage. As Kierkegaard put it, "to venture is to face anxiety, but not to venture is to lose oneself."

MASTER TIME AND ACTIVITY FORM

DAILY ACTIVITY PLANNING   DATE _____

Communications	Activities
1. Meetings and Isolation Time	**2. Most Dominant** **(must be done today)**
8:00	
9:00	
10:00	
11:00	
12:00	
1:00	
2:00	
3:00	
4:00	
5:00	
6:00	
Evening	
4. Interpersonal Investment Other people to see, telephone, or write to	**3. Activities to Promote** **More Deferrable Objectives**

5. Personal Revitalization Activities

_____

_____

_____

_____

_____